*To Melissa
and in memory of my parents*

Contents

Lesson 1 Cold Feet   1

get cold feet • can/can't afford • have second thoughts • deep down • get/be married • tie the knot • get hitched • can/can't tell • read *someone's* mind • be a mind reader • shoot • for good • history repeats itself • be through • be dying to • have *something* in common • cut out • be chicken • chicken out • wind up

Lesson 2 Guess Who?   14

in ages • for ages • be on the way • be out of the way • be in the way • come on • get going • drop in • drop by • stop by • drop off • pick up • drop out • feel free • keep in touch • lose touch • be in/out of touch • get back in touch • run into • bump into

Lesson 3 Please Leave a Message After You Hear the Beep   23

please leave a message after you hear the beep/tone • check one's messages • a pain • a pain in the neck • go/be out of one's mind • go nuts/bananas • go off one's rocker • hang up • write *something* down • going on • stand still • get up the nerve • freeze • get/be tongue-tied • do *something* on one's own/by oneself • be just about ready to • good for you • don't be silly • have a seat • wish me luck • take a deep breath • be out of breath • have bad breath • here goes

Lesson 4 In Bad Shape   36

catch/have a cold • catch/have the flu • I have news for you • be in the same boat • keep *someone* company • all day/night long • can't stop • I know what you mean • take *someone's* temperature • sound like • chances are • get over • be in good/bad shape • feel sorry for

Acknowledgments

I would like to thank all of my editors, colleagues, friends, and family members who provided me with support, encouragement, and valuable feedback as I worked on this second edition of *All Clear*.

I especially appreciate the wonderful working relationship that I've had since the early 1980s with members of the Heinle & Heinle staff. As I've watched the company expand in ESL over the years, I've been extremely impressed with how it has remained a friendly, warm, and really personal organization. I am grateful to Heinle & Heinle for encouraging me to write the second edition of *All Clear,* an endeavor that has been both a great challenge and pleasure.

Thank you to everyone involved with the actual production of this book: Dave Lee, Kristin Thalheimer, Rachel Youngman, Talbot Hamlin, and Brian Orr. And to my ESL colleagues—Kathi Jordan, Amy Prentiss, and Cynthia Weber, I would like to express my great appreciation for your willingness to field test the new material and provide me with such valuable feedback.

To my friends, thank you for your first names for the dialogues.

To my daughter, thank you for giving me your "gut" native speaker responses to my questions—you helped me make sure that I was keeping the language natural.

To ESL/EFL students, thank you for your enthusiasm for learning idioms and your questions about their meanings and use. In this text, I have made a great effort to anticipate and answer your questions.

And to everyone who uses "Son of All Clear," as Dave Lee once called it, I hope you have a great time and laugh a lot.

Helen Fragiadakis

To the Student

To understand what an *idiom* is, take a look at the pictures below:

Steve *ran into* Melissa yesterday.

Literal meaning =
They crashed into each other

Idiomatic meaning =
They met without planning

For both pictures, we can say that "Steve *ran into* Melissa yesterday." In the first picture, that sentence means that Steve was running and then crashed into Melissa, and maybe even hurt her. In the second picture, that sentence means that Steve and Melissa met each other without planning to meet. When they saw each other, they were surprised.

"*Ran into*" in the second picture is an *idiom*. An idiom is a group of words with a special meaning. This idiom means "to meet someone without planning to meet." It does not mean that anyone was running.

Write down two idioms from your native language:

1. _____   2. _____

Translate these into English for your classmates, and then tell the class the meaning of each of your idioms.

You will study many idioms in this book, but you will also study *formulas*. Formulas are "set" expressions that do not change. These expressions are used in specific situations. Formulas are NOT idioms because their words do not have a special meaning when they are put together. Here are some examples of formulas:

It's nice to meet you.
Excuse me.
See you later.

As you learn the new vocabulary in this book, you will have many opportunities to improve your listening and speaking skills. Good luck, and have a great time!

Introduction to the Teacher

ALL CLEAR! is an intermediate/advanced level ESL or EFL text that:

— teaches students to recognize and produce high-frequency American idioms and formulas,

— provides numerous contexts from which students can infer meanings,

— furnishes examples of natural conversation (in print and on the audio program) that cover a wide range of speech acts and emotions,

— exposes students to conversational situations reflecting social customs that can serve as a basis for cross-cultural discussions and

— provides many structured and communicative activities for listening and speaking practice.

For those who are familiar with the first edition, the main changes that have been made in the second edition include:

— Six new lessons (the odd-numbered lessons) with updated contexts.

— More definitions of idioms.

— New, more sophisticated, and contemporary cartoons.

— New dictations.

— More communicative activities.

Organization of Each Lesson

— Opening dialogue—A lively, *natural* conversation enhanced by an amusing illustration.

— Comprehension and culturally based discussion questions related to the opening dialogue.

— "Understanding the New Expressions" section, in which new vocabulary is presented in mini-dialogues so as to provide additional contexts for students. In addition, similar, related, and contrasting expressions are introduced, along with grammatical and other pertinent information.

—Eight exercises, at first structured, and then more communicative. (These are explained in detail in "Suggested Teaching Methods" on page xv.)

Review Games

A crossword puzzle, a tic tac toe game, and a "Guess the Idiom" exercise appear at the end of each set of four lessons, providing reinforcement and review in an enjoyable context. Specific instructions for presenting the games appear in the "Suggested Teaching Methods" section.

Answer Key

Appendix B contains the answers to Exercises 1 and 2 for all lessons. Appendix C contains the answers to the crossword puzzles and "Guess the Idiom" exercises in the Review Games.

Audio Program

The supplementary audio program (available in both cassette tape and compact disc) contains the opening dialogue, the Exercise 2 "Choosing the Idiom" dialogue, and the dictation from each lesson.

Each dialogue is first performed as it appears in the text. Then it is presented again with pauses so that students can repeat, phrase by phrase, what the speakers say.

The dictations are presented just as they would be by the teacher in class. First, the entire dictation is read as the students listen. Second, students write as they are given the dictation. Third, students check what they have written as they again listen to the dictation.

Suggested Teaching Methods

Following are many detailed suggestions for presenting the components of ALL CLEAR! in class.

Suggested Teaching Methods

Opening Dialogue

Call students' attention to the headphone symbol at the left of the dialogue. Point out that this symbol means that this material is on the audio program.

Depending on the time available and the level of your students, you might choose to do only some of the following steps.

A. *Dialogue covered:* students look only at the illustration (which can be shown on a transparency).

1. Ask students to look at the illustration and describe what they think the situation is and what they think the characters are saying to each other. Have them comment on facial expressions, gestures, and the physical distances between the speakers. (If you have the time, students can do this in small groups.)
2. Play the audio program while students look at the illustration. If the audio program is not available, you can dramatize the dialogue yourself.

B. *Dialogue uncovered or on an overhead transparency.*

1. Have students read the dialogue as you play the audio program again.
2. Have students repeat the lines of the dialogue.
3. Ask the questions that follow the dialogue. Discuss the social customs, speech acts, and emotions portrayed, and compare them to how they are handled in the students' native cultures.
4. Ask students to summarize what transpired in the dialogue.
5. Have students practice reading the dialogue aloud in pairs.

Understanding the New Expressions

1. Model each new expression for students and have them note which words are stressed. Have students repeat the expressions after you.
2. Discuss each new vocabulary item with the class. In this section, mini-dialogues dramatize the uses of each expression in appropriate contexts.
3. Go over the additional expressions presented along with the idioms and formulas being studied. These similar, contrasting, and otherwise related expressions enrich students' vocabulary.

Exercises

Exercises can be done individually, in pairs, or in groups. It would be best to have the students do the Lesson 1 exercises in class so that you can help them become accustomed to the format. From then on, they should be able to do at least Exercises 1 and 2 for homework. An answer key for Exercises 1 and 2 is provided in Appendix B.

Exercises 4 and 8 are adaptations of the "One-Minute Paper" and "Applications Cards" techniques explained in K. Patricia Cross's and Thomas A. Angelo's handbook for faculty called *Classroom Assessment Techniques*. This handbook was published by the National Center for Research to Improve Postsecondary Teaching and Learning (NCRIPTL), University of Michigan, Ann Arbor, Michigan.

The following is a description of each exercise:

1. Mini-Dialogues—A matching exercise giving students practice in using idioms in very brief conversational exchanges. The best way to check this exercise in class is to have one student read an item from column A aloud and then have another student read the appropriate response from column B so that everyone can hear the mini-dialogues that are created through matching.

2. Choosing the Idiom—A fill-in-the-blank dialogue accompanied by a word list and an illustration. This exercise gives students a chance to see some of the idioms used in another context. Also, when providing answers, students learn to give attention to grammatical factors such as subject-verb agreement and verb tense.

3. Dictation—Dictation of a short paragraph, often containing reported speech, that summarizes the opening dialogue. It would be best to use the audio program to give the dictation, but if that is not possible, the dictations can be read from Appendix A.

Be sure that students know the words for punctuation marks: period, comma, question mark, exclamation point, dash hyphen, colon, semi-colon. They should also know what "indent" means.

Dictation Directions

a. While students just listen, read the entire dictation aloud at normal speed, using natural stress and intonation.
b. Give the dictation, pausing at natural points between phrases and sentences while students write. Include the necessary punctuation as you dictate.
c. Read the entire dictation once more so that students can check their work.
d. To check students' work:
   —Collect the dictations or
   —Have students exchange papers and circle errors as they look at the corrected dictation on the board, on an overhead transparency, or in Appendix A.

4. Any Questions?—A classroom assessment technique that gives you an opportunity midway through the exercises to get anonymous feedback from students about the highlights and confusing aspects of each lesson. Actually, this activity can be done at any time during a lesson. You should collect the papers, and at the next class meeting distribute a handout with a list of the questions that came up, or write the list on the board or on a transparency. The questions can be answered by (a) you, (b) students you call on, or (c) students in small groups. The real purpose of this activity is to reach the quieter students who may hesitate to ask questions.

5. *Personal Questions*—Questions (containing new vocabulary) related to students' personal lives. This exercise is best done orally, but it can be written. Students can work in pairs or small groups to answer these questions.

This can also be done as a "Hot Seat" activity. Choose one student to be on the Hot Seat—this student has to answer all the questions in front of the whole class. Classmates take turns asking the "Personal Questions."

6. *Skit Writing*—Student- or class-written dialogues based on specific situations, accompanied by illustrations. This activity should culminate in groups of students practicing and then performing their skits in front of the class.

You may wish to follow the steps listed below before having students do this exercise on their own:

1. For the first lesson: Write the dialogue as a class. Have students look at the illustration and offer suggested lines for the dialogue while you write the lines on the board. Point out the problem if one utterance does not logically follow another, so that students see immediately that coherence is an important factor in writing dialogues. Discuss grammatical changes that need to be made in the expressions (tense, person, pronoun, etc.)

2. For the second lesson: Have students write the dialogues in pairs while you circulate, offering help as needed.

3. For the subsequent lessons: Intersperse the methods suggested above with opportunities for students to write the dialogues individually. Type up (corrected) student-written dialogues for the entire class. These will portray the new expressions in many different contexts.

7. *Improvisation*—Role-plays based on situations that elicit the use of specific idiomatic expressions. This exercise is completely oral, *not* written.

The following steps are suggested:

1. You or a student writes the expressions on the board. It is convenient to refer to the Contents when doing this.
2. Add any other expressions that you would like to review. Be sure that they somehow fit into the contexts of the suggested role-plays.
3. Put students into small groups and give them time to briefly (and orally) prepare what they will say. Suggested first lines are provided. Be sure that they understand the context of the role-play. If you have a chance to bring in props beforehand, give them out now.
4. Have one group of students come to the front of the class. Remind the group to glance periodically at the board in order to include at least some of the new expressions.
5. As they perform, you can:
   — note which idioms were used and plan to comment on how they were pro-

nounced and whether or not they were used correctly in terms of grammar and context,

— videotape the students. The tape can then be replayed for the entire class or privately for only those who performed.

8. Real Life—Another classroom assessment technique that encourages the transfer of expressions from the classroom to the outside world. Students list at least five new expressions and then write down where and with whom they might use these expressions in their own lives. They can share these lists in small groups, or you can collect and type up the lists. You might even have the students write mini-dialogues that represent conversations with their relatives and friends.

It is always useful to ask students if they ever use or hear the expressions previously studied, and if they say yes, to ask where they were used or heard, and who was speaking.

Review Games

I   Crossword Puzzles

Crossword puzzles require students to supply parts of expressions with the correct spelling. Students unfamiliar with this activity will need "across" and "down" explained. Puzzle solutions appear in *Appendix C*.

II   Tic Tac Toe

Tic Tac Toe requires students to produce grammatically and semantically correct sentences containing the new expressions.

Steps to Tic Tac Toe

1. First play a traditional Tic Tac Toe game so that students become familiar with the strategy involved. Explain that any straight line wins, whether it is horizontal, vertical, or diagonal.
2. Put the Tic Tac Toe grid on the board, and fill in the spaces with expressions to be reviewed.
3. Divide the class into two teams X and O. Flip a coin (and teach "heads or tails") to see which team will start.
4. To get an X or an O in a space, a team has to create a grammatically and semantically correct sentence using the expression which appears there. Allow team members to confer, but give a 30-second time limit. Be sure students take turns giving the answers.
5. The first team to get three X's or O's in a straight line wins.
6. If there are any expressions left uncovered by X's or O's, keep them for another game. Add other expressions to the spaces already used, and play again.

III   Guess the Idiom

For fun, students guess which idioms are portrayed in pictures representing the literal interpretations of the expressions.

Pronunciation Practice

In each lesson, the opening dialogue and the dialogue in Exercise 2, "Choosing the Idiom," can provide contexts for pronunciation practice. On the audio program, each dialogue is read twice. The first time, the dialogue is performed at natural speed. The second time, it is read with pauses so that students can repeat what they have heard.

If you would like to use these dialogues as contexts for special pronunciation work, you may want to consider the following:

A. Reduced forms

Look for reduced forms in each dialogue (e.g., "Why don't you?"—"Why doncha?") Students do not need to actually pronounce the reduced forms, but it is very important that they learn to recognize them when they are used by native speakers.

B. Linking

Have students practice linking words within phrases. For example, in "I wish I could," the words "wish" and "I" sound like one word, "wishay."

C. Stress

1. Have students pronounce each new expression with the correct stress.
2. If students have learned the basic rules for sentence stress, have them mark all the words in the dialogue that should be stressed. Have them perform the dialogue. Correct stress errors only.

D. Intonation

If students have learned the basic rules for rising and falling intonation, have them mark the intonation lines on their dialogues. This can vary in detail; you may want them to mark only question intonation.

E. -ed and -s word endings

1. If students have studied the rules for the pronunciation of these suffixes, have them circle the words in the dialogue which demonstrate the use of these rules.

2. For -ed pronunciation, have the students list all of the regular verbs that appear in the dialogue. Have them put those verbs into the past tense, and then pronounce the verbs.

3. For -s pronunciation, have students list all of the countable nouns that appear in the dialogue. Have them make them plural (if they aren't plural already), and then pronounce those words.

4. For further -s pronunciation, have students list all of the verbs that appear in the dialogue, put them into third person singular, and then pronounce the verbs.

F. Vowel and consonant pronunciation and/or contrasts

If in pronunciation you are focusing, for example, on the vowel /au/ as in "cow," or the two "th" sounds, have the students circle these sounds in the dialogue. When they perform the dialogue, correct only the mispronunciation of these sounds.

Applying A through F in class

The following is a specific example of how to connect some of the above aspects of pronunciation with part of an actual dialogue from Lesson 8 of this text. The dialogue is marked to demonstrate what students would write in response to the directions below.

Partial dialogue from Lesson 8

Rosemary: Hello?

Frank: Hi Rosemary. This is Frank. How're you doing?

Rosemary: OK, but busy.

Frank: Can you make time to go to a movie this afternoon?

Rosemary: I wish I could, but I have a lot of homework. I'll have to take a rain check.

Frank: Come on, take some time off. You're always studying! You're going to turn

            into a robot before you know it.

Rosemary: Well, I have a lot to do. Don't you have work to do?

Frank: I did, but I got it over with, so I can leave early.

Directions that you can give students:

1. Circle all of the words with the "th" sound.
2. The following are reduced forms: How're you . . .?   (How—er—ya . . .?)
                                       to go to a . . .?   (ta—go—da—a . . .)
                                       going to   (gonna or going ta . . .)
                                       Don't you . . .?   (Doncha . . .?)

   Underline these in the dialogue.

3. The words in the following phrases should be linked. That means that you should say them as if they were one word.

   This is . . .   Come on . . .
   wish I . . .   time off . . .
   but I . . .   have a . . .
   take a . . .   got it over . . .

   Draw a ‿ that shows these words are linked in the dialogue.

4. There are four questions in the dialogue. Which use rising intonation, and which use rising-falling intonation? Why? Mark the intonation for these questions.

   (Rising intonation—"Hello?" and the Yes-No questions, "Can you make time to
                                                            go to . . .?
                                                            "Don't you have work
                                                            to do?"

   Rising-falling intonation—WH question, "How're you doing?")

5. Mark the stressed words in the sentences, "I wish I could, but I have a lot of homework. I'll have to take a rain check."

Covering all of these pronunciation points in one lesson would, of course, be confusing and counterproductive; choose as many as you think your students can handle at one time. The key point here is that the dialogues in this text provide useful contexts for practicing whatever you want to cover in pronunciation. By making students sensitive to correct pronunciation, you will help them gain the experience of monitoring themselves as they perform the dialogues and participate in real-life conversations.

A Note About the Terminology Used in This Text

In this book, *two-word verbs* are labeled *separable* or *inseparable* and *transitive* or *intransitive*. The following explains the meanings of these terms.

Two-word verb = verb + another word, such as: to *get over* a cold,
to *drop in*

Separable vs. Inseparable:

Separable two-word verbs can be separated by direct objects:

He figured out his problem.   He figured his problem out.

When the direct object is a pronoun, it must be inserted *between* the two parts of the verb:

He figured out his problem.   He figured it out.

He figured out it. (incorrect)

Inseparable two-word verbs cannot be separated by direct objects:

She got over her cold.
She got her cold over. (incorrect)

Transitive vs. Intransitive:

Transitive two-word verbs must have direct objects; intransitive two-word verbs do not have direct objects. Since direct objects are required to form the passive voice, only transitive verbs can be put into the passive:

Transitive: They figured out the problem. (the problem = direct object)
The problem was figured out (by them). (passive voice)

Intransitive: The movie gets out at 11:00. (no direct object)
(passive voice not possible).

Cold Feet

ELLEN: Can you believe it? Your wedding is in two weeks!

JANA: And I think I'm **getting cold feet.**

ELLEN: Why? What are you afraid of? Rick's a great guy.

JANA: I know, but maybe we should wait. We **can't** even **afford to** buy furniture!

ELLEN: So, it's money that's making you **have second thoughts. Deep down** you really want to **get married. I can tell** by your face—you really love him.

JANA: Ellen, sometimes I think you can **read my mind.**

❖ ❖ ❖ ❖ ❖

RICK: Tim, can I ask you a question?

TIM: **Shoot!**

RICK: Do you think I'm ready to get married?

TIM: That's a strange question. Are you **getting cold feet?**

RICK: I guess you could say that. I was thinking, you know, marriage is **for good,** and I don't want to make a mistake. There are so many divorces these days and . . . my parents are divorced, you know. **History repeats itself** a lot and . . .

1

TIM: **Are** you **through?** Do you have any more reasons why you shouldn't marry Jana?

RICK: But I'm **dying to** marry her.

TIM: Do you want my advice? You and Jana **have a lot in common.** You're perfect for each other. So **cut out** all this nonsense and don't **be** so **chicken.** If you **wind up without** Jana, you'll be sorry.

QUESTIONS
1. How do Jana and Rick feel about getting married?
2. What do you think "to get cold feet" means?
3. If you are married, did you get cold feet before your wedding? Explain.
   If you are not married, do you think you will get cold feet before your wedding?

■ Understanding the New Expressions

Note: *S1 and S2 refer to Speaker 1 and Speaker 2.*

1. **get (or have) cóld féet** = become so nervous about starting something new (such as a marriage or a new job) that you think you shouldn't do it

   S1: Your new job starts soon, doesn't it?
   S2: Uh-huh, but the problem is, I'm **getting cold feet** and thinking that I should call them and tell them to look for someone else.
   S1: You really wanted that job. Why would you do that?
   S2: Well, they want someone who knows a lot about computers, and I know some, but not a lot.

   S1: Didn't they get married?
   S2: No. At the last minute, she **got cold feet** and canceled the wedding.

2. **can/cán't affórd to *do something*** or
   can/cán't affórd *something* = have or not have enough money to buy something

   S1: I didn't know you had a job.
   S2: Well, I **can't afford to** go to school full-time. So I work and go to school part-time.

   S1: I thought you were going to buy a new car.
   S2: I wanted to, but I **couldn't afford** one. I had to get a used car, but it's OK.

   S1: That video camera is so expensive!
   S2: Don't worry. I **can afford** it.

3. **have sécond thóughts** = think that your decision may not be a good one
   have second thoughts about *doing something*
   have second thoughts about *something or someone*

2

S1: I'll buy it.
S2: Are you sure? No **second thoughts?**
S1: No **second thoughts.** Here's my check.

S1: I need to talk to you. I'm **having second thoughts about buying** that car.
S2: What's the problem?
S1: Well, first of all, it's really expensive. And second of all, it's an automatic, and I'd rather have a manual transmission.

S1: They're **having second thoughts about** that house.
S2: What do you mean?
S1: Well, it's an old house and they're afraid that they'll have a lot of problems if they live there.

S1: What do you think of the new guy?
S2: I'm afraid I'm **having second thoughts about** him. At first, I was sure he was right for the job, but now I'm not so sure. His work isn't as good as I expected.

4. **déep dówn** = deep in your heart—your true feelings

S1: I told them that I wanted to fly, but **deep down** I'd really like to drive.
S2: Why?
S1: I've never told anyone this before, but I'm afraid of flying.

S1: Look at how they are all smiling at each other. But **deep down** they really don't like each other.
S2: How do you know?
S1: Trust me. I know.

5. **gét márried (to)** = become married; marry;
go through the process of becoming married

S1: When are you **getting married?**
S2: In a month or two.

S1: They're married?
S2: Yup (yes). They **got married** last year.

Similar (but very informal) expressions: tie the knot/get hitched

—When are you two going to **tie the knot?**
—When are you two going to **get hitched?**

—They **tied the knot** last year.
—They **got hitched** last year.

Contrast: be married (to) = after people **get** married, then they **are** married

S1: Did you know that Rick **is married** to Jana?
S2: That's great.

S1: Listen, everyone. We have a surprise for you. We**'re married!**
S2: Really? Congratulations!

Note: *People* **get married** *at their wedding. Then they* **are married.**
They are married "to" each other, not "with" each other.

Related expressions with verbs:

> **be engaged (to** *someone***)**
> **split up** = **separate** (before getting a divorce)
> **break up (with** *someone***)** = **end a relationship**
> **be separated (from** *someone***)**
> **divorce someone/get a divorce (from** *someone***)**
> **be divorced (from** *someone***)**
> **remarry** = **marry again; get married again**
> **be remarried**
> **get back together (with** *someone***)**

Related nouns:

> **a wedding** = the ceremony in which people get married
> **a reception** = the party after the ceremony
> **a marriage** = a relationship between a man and woman in which the
> man is the husband and the woman is the wife.
> We can say: a good/bad marriage
> a happy/an unhappy marriage
> a perfect marriage
> a "marriage made in heaven"
> **fiancé** = a man to whom a woman is engaged
> **fiancée** = a woman to whom a man is engaged
> **marital status** = this is often asked on official forms. It means: Are you
> married or single? If you are married, your marital status is "married." If
> you are single, your marital status is "single." In the past, "divorced"
> was also considered marital status, but today a divorced person can
> be considered "single."

6. *(someone)* **can/cán't téll (by)** = be able or not be able to see or hear what something really is

S1: Can you **tell** that I was crying? Are my eyes red?
S2: No, I **can't tell.** No one will notice, so don't worry.

S1: There's a new driver in front of us.
S2: How do you know?
S1: I **can tell by** the way he's sitting, and how slowly he's driving.

S1: Can you read this? The handwriting is so bad that I **can't tell** what it says.
S2: Neither can I.

7. **réad** *someone's* **mínd** = know what someone is really thinking
be a mínd reader = be someone who knows what others are thinking

S1: This party isn't very exciting. You want to go home, don't you?
S2: Are you **reading my mind?**

S1: You knew I didn't want to fly. Why didn't we drive?
S2: How could I know that you didn't want to fly?
Do you think I can **read your mind?**
or
Do you think I can **read minds?**
or
Do you think I'**m a mind reader?**

8. **Shóot!** = a friendly, very informal way to let others know that they are free to ask you a question

S1: There's something that I've been wanting to ask you.
S2: Shoot!
S1: How old are you?

S1: Can I ask you a question?
S2: Sure. **Shoot!**

Cold Feet

9. for góod = forever, permanently

S1: Our marriage is over **for good.** I don't want to talk about it.
S2: But you have to talk. This is important.

S1: I just got a letter from my son—finally.
S2: Any news?
S1: Yeah-big news. He's coming home **for good.** You know-he's been traveling for over two years?
S2: That long? Well then he probably really wants to come home by now.

10. hístory répeats itself = this is an expression or "saying" that means that something that happened in the past happens or may happen again because we don't "learn from our mistakes"

S1: I hope there won't be another war.
S2: So do I. We never seem to learn from the mistakes of the past so **history** always **repeats itself.** It's crazy.

11. be thróugh (with *something*) = be finished (with something)

S1: Can you help me?
S2: Sure. I'll **be through** in a second.

S1: When **we're through with** our homework, do you want to take a walk?
S2: That sounds like a great idea. I need to get out for a little while.

Note: *If you use a verb after "through with," make sure that you use the verb + ing (gerund). When you use "through + gerund, the word "with" is optional.*

—When I'**m through (with) doing** the dishes, I'll take a shower.

Note: *When you are **through** with something, you are finished with an activity that you were actively doing. When something is **over** (such as a movie), it is finished, but you have no control over it.*

Note: *Be careful with words that have similar spelling:*
thorough = complete; thought = past tense of think; taught = past tense of teach

12. be dýing to do *something* = want to do something very, very much

S1: That new movie is finally here. I'**m dying to** see it. Want to come?
S2: What's it about?

S1: Why are you going home so early?
S2: I'**m dying to** get the mail. I'm expecting something kind of special.

6

> **be dýing of thírst** = be very, very thirsty
> **be dýing of húnger** = be very, very hungry

—It's so hot and I'**m dying of thirst.** Let's stop and get a drink.
—I haven't eaten since this morning and I'**m dying of hunger.**

13. **have a lót/a líttle/véry líttle/nóthing in cómmon** (with someone) = share or not share the same interests

S1: Let's introduce Marie to Tom. I think they'd like each other.
S2: Great idea. They **have a lot in common,** don't you think?

S1: Let's introduce Fran to Andrew. I think they'd like each other.
S2: I don't think so. They **have nothing in common** (with each other). I'm surprised that you thought they'd like each other. I think we should introduce Andrew to Valerie.

14. **cút óut** *something* or **cút** *something* **óut** (separable/transitive) = stop some behavior

S1: Hey—**cut out** all that noise in there!
S2: Too bad! Close the door.

S1: You'd better **cut out** smoking because it is really bad for you.
S2: You're right. Anyway, there aren't many places left where it's legal to smoke.

Note: *This is an **informal** expression. The first dialogue above would probably be spoken by close family members. The second dialogue might take place between two friends or between a doctor and a patient.*

People who know each other very well might say, when they are angry about something someone is doing:

—Cút thát oút! or
—Cút it óut!

Contrast: **cút** *something* **óut** (**of** *something*) = with scissors or a knife, cut something out of a larger piece

S1: My mother would be interested in this newspaper article.
S2: Why don't you **cut** it **out of** the paper and send it to her?

S1: How did you make that beautiful paper doll?
S2 (child): I drew a picture on a big piece of paper and then I **cut** it **out.**

15. **be chícken** = be afraid

S1: Jump! Come on—you can do it.
S2: No, I'**m** too **chicken.** It's too far and I know I'll fall.

Similar expression: **be a chícken** = be a person who is afraid

S1: Go tell him!
S2: Ssh! No. I**'m a chicken.** You tell him.

Similar expression: **to chícken óut** (inseparable/intransitive) = not to do something that you planned to do because you became afraid

S1: Did you tell him?
S2: No, I **chickened out.**

Note: These idioms with the word "chicken" are often used by children when they try to make (force) each other do something. Adults however, sometimes use these expressions in informal situations.

16. **wínd úp with** *or* **without** *something* (inseparable/transitive) = end up = finish by becoming something else

S1: If you don't take better care of yourself, you'll **wind up with** a cold.
S2: All right. I'll take my jacket.

S1: They gambled all their money and **wound up without** a cent.
S2: *All* their money?

Similar expression: **wínd úp** + _____ **ing**
                                        verb

S1: If we don't make a decision soon, we'll **wind up going** nowhere.
S2: Why don't we just go to the beach?

Contrast: **wínd úp (** *an object* **)** (separable/transitive) = turn in a circular motion so that something (an object) will be able to work

—In the past, if we didn't **wind up** our watches every day, they would stop working. But now, most watches have batteries, so we don't have to **wind** them **up.**

1. Mini-Dialogues

Below are two columns, A and B. Column A contains the first lines of dialogues and column B contains possible responses. For each opening line in column A, choose the *best* response from column B.

When checking this exercise in class, perform each mini-dialogue. One student should read an item from column A and another student should respond with the answer from column B.

A

_____ **1.** Can I ask you a question?

_____ **2.** Let's watch TV.

_____ **3.** He has two cars and a boat and he works in a fast food restaurant.

_____ **4.** I'm dying of thirst.

_____ **5.** I'm telling them what you told me.

_____ **6.** I thought you were going to make a speech in front of all the teachers.

_____ **7.** Listen—I've got some interesting news for you.

_____ **8.** Are they laughing or crying?

_____ **9.** Let me try to read your mind. You are thinking about breaking up.

_____ **10.** What are you doing here? I thought you'd be away by now.

_____ **11.** All right, I'll do it.

_____ **12.** What is your marital status?

_____ **13.** I'm not staying here for good. I want to see the world.

_____ **14.** The same thing happened a hundred years ago.

_____ **15.** I like music, dancing, sports and reading.

_____ **16.** I'm sorry I'm so chicken, but I'm afraid of dogs.

_____ **17.** She wasn't a good student, but she wound up becoming a successful businesswoman.

B

a. I almost did, but I got cold feet.

b. No, you're wrong! I'm thinking about getting married.

c. I can't now, but I'll be able to when I'm through.

d. I can't tell.

e. No, don't. I know that deep down you don't really want to. I'll find someone else to do it.

f. I always thought she was smart.

g. I know, but I had second thoughts when I realized how expensive the trip would be.

h. Why don't you stop complaining and get yourself a glass of water?

i. It looks like we have a lot in common.

j. How can he afford those things?

k. Cut it out! I told you not to tell anyone. Can't you keep a secret?

l. Single.

m. You know how it is. History always repeats itself because people don't learn from their mistakes.

n. Do your parents know what you want to do?

o. Sure. Shoot!

p. Hurry up and tell me. I'm dying to hear.

q. No problem. I'll put him outside.

2. Choosing the Idiom

The following dialogue takes place between the two people in the illustration. Fill in the blanks with some of the expressions on the list. Pay special attention to how the expressions are used grammatically. (You will need to consider verb tenses, subject-verb agreement, plurals, etc.) After you have checked your answers, perform the dialogue with a partner.

have a lot in common	can tell	cold feet
be dying to	through	(not) have second thoughts
read my mind	shoot	deep down
for good	chicken	get married

TIM: Still have _____ ?
(1)

RICK: No. And I _____ either. I feel great.
(2)

TIM: I _____ . You look really happy. So does Jana.
(3)

RICK: Where is she? Did you see her?

TIM: Oh, yeah. But you can't until the ceremony.

RICK: That's a crazy superstition. Show me where she is.

I _____ see her.
(4)

TIM: Oh, no. Her mother would be really mad. She told me that on the day people _____ (5) _____ , they shouldn't see each other

'til the ceremony.

RICK: I don't think that Jana's mother and I _____ (6) _____ .

But _____ (7) _____ , I really like her. I hope she likes

me.

TIM: I'm sure she does. She was just saying that when

she's _____ (8) _____ helping Jana, she'll come down

and look for you to see how you're doing. How are you doing?

RICK: That's a good question. What time is it?

3. Dictation

Your teacher or one of your classmates will read the dictation for this unit from Appendix A, or you will listen to the dictation on the audio program. You will hear the dictation three times. First, just listen. Second, as you listen, write the dictation on a separate sheet of paper. Third, as you listen, check what you have written.

4. Any Questions?

Take out a piece of paper. Do NOT write your name on it. On one side of the paper, write down what you think is the most interesting information that you have learned in this lesson up to now. On the other side of the paper, write down any questions that you have about any of the idioms. Your teacher will collect this paper and then answer your questions the next time you meet.

5. Personal Questions

Answer the questions below in a conversation with a partner or in a small group.

1. Talk about a time when you had plans, but then got cold feet. (Perhaps you were going to get married, start a new school or job, take a big trip, try a dangerous sport, or say something serious to someone.)

2. As you can see from the dialogue in Exercise 2, some American people have superstitions about getting married. Discuss superstitions related to wedding customs in your native country.

3. Deep down, do you *really* want to learn English, or are you studying it because: (a) your school requires it, (b) your parents want you to learn it, or (c) it is necessary for your work? Explain your answer.

4. What is something that you are dying to do within the next five years?

5. When we say that "history repeats itself," we mean that we don't learn from the mistakes of the past, so we keep making the same mistakes. Is there an expression in your native language that has the same or a similar meaning?

6. In English, a chicken is someone who is afraid to do something, and a pig is someone who doesn't eat with good manners. In your native language, are people ever called by animal names? If yes, when? What do you say?

6. Skit Writing

In this illustration, Rick's and Jana's friends, Tim and Ellen, are at the reception after the wedding ceremony. They are talking about how happy their friends are now that they are married. They also tell each other about the conversation they each had in the swimming pool when Jana told Ellen and Rick told Tim about *having cold feet*. Tim starts the conversation by asking Ellen "Did you know that Rick had cold feet?"

Work individually, in pairs, or as a class to write their conversation. Try to use at least five new expressions from this lesson. After you have finished, perform the "skit" you created for your class.

7. Improvisation

Using the new expressions from this lesson, act out the following role-play. The new expressions should be written on the board.

Your life is about to change. You are going to get married, move to a new city (or country), and start a new job. But there's a problem—you are having second thoughts. You really like where you live now, and you already have a good job. What should you do?

Discuss this problem with a close friend. This close friend will ask you many questions and then give you advice. The question is: Will you follow your friend's advice or not? *You* decide.

Possible starting lines:
FRIEND (concerned advisor):   What's wrong? You look upset.
YOU (worried):   I am. I . . .

8. Real Life

Think of situations in your own life in which you might use some of the expressions from this lesson. Write down at least five. Outside of class, remember your list and try to use some of your new vocabulary. Also, when you watch TV and listen to people speak, listen carefully—you may hear these expressions.

Expressions	*Real-Life Situations*
Example: *can't afford to*	*I would say this a lot—when shopping, looking at ads in newspapers and magazines, when talking to friends about things I need, want or dream about doing.*

1.

2.

3.

4.

5.

Guess Who?

PETER: Guess who?

LAURA: José? No, not José. Peter! I can't believe it! I haven't seen you **in ages.** How are you?

PETER: Pretty good.

LAURA: Can you join me?

PETER: I wish I could, but I'**m on my way** out. I have to be in the city in an hour.

LAURA: **Come on.** Just for a minute.

PETER: There's a lot of traffic and I really have to **get going.** Listen, you know where I live—why don't you **drop in** one evening?

LAURA: I'll do that. And **feel free to drop in on** me, too. Let's **keep in touch.**

PETER: I'd really like to. Talk to you soon. I'm glad I **ran into** you. Take care.

QUESTIONS 1. Is it customary in your native country for someone to cover a friend's eyes and say, "Guess who?"

2. During their conversation, the two friends hug each other. Would this happen in your native country? Would two men hug? Do parents hug and kiss their children? Why or why not?

3. Is it acceptable in your native country to visit somebody without calling first?

■ Understanding the New Expressions

1. **in áges/for áges** = in a long time

S1: How's Tony these days?
S2: I don't know. I haven't seen him **in/for ages.**

Note: *When "in ages" and "for ages" mean "in a long time," they are used in negative sentences.*

Contrast: **for áges** = for a long time

S1: We've been in this traffic **for ages.**
S2: We sure have. I want to go home.

Note: *"In ages" and "for ages" are usually used with verbs in the present perfect tense.*

2. **be ón one's wáy/be ón the wáy (to)** = be in the process of going somewhere

S1: Where are you?
S2: I'm { **on my way** home.
　　　　 on the way

S1: Hi, is Mollie there?
S2: Is this Heather? No, she just left. She's { **on her way to** your house.
　　　　　　　　　　　　　　　　　　　 on the way to

Contrast: be óut of one's wáy, be ín one's wáy, be ín the wáy

S1: I can stop at the store before I pick you up.
S2: No, don't. The store **is out of your way** and we don't have time.

S1: I can't see the movie. That tall guy's head **is** { **in my way.**
{ **in the way.**

S2: Tell him to move his head { **out of your way.**
{ **out of the way.**

3. Come ón.

   Encouraging:

   S1: I really can't stay.
   S2: Come on. Stay for five minutes

   S1: I'll never learn English.
   S2: Come on. That's no way to talk.

   Hurrying:

   —**Come on.** We're late.

   Expressing disbelief:

   —**Come on.** I don't believe you.

4. gét góing = leave

   S1: The movie starts in twenty minutes. We'd better **get going.**
   S2: I'll be right there.

5. dróp ín = dróp bý = stóp bý *(all inseparable/intransitive)* = visit

   S1: There's Peter's house. Let's **drop by** and surprise him.
   S2: I don't think it's a good idea to **drop in** without calling first.
   S1: I think it's OK to **stop by.**

   Similar expressions:

   dróp ín at *(a place)* *(inseparable/transitive)*
   dróp ín on *(a person)* *(inseparable/transitive)*

   S1: Let's **drop in at** Peter's house.
   S2: That's a good idea. It would be fun to **drop in on** him.

   Contrast: dróp óff ≠ píck úp *(separable/transitive)*

   S1: I have to **drop** my sweater **off** at the cleaners today so I can **pick it up** tomorrow.
   S2: I'll **drop** you **off** at the corner.

Contrast:

>**dróp óut of** *(a place or activity)* *(inseparable/transitive)*
>**dróp óut** *(inseparable/intransitive)*
>**(be a) drópout**

S1: He **dropped out of** school last year and he still can't find a job.
S2: He **dropped out** last year?
S1: Yes, it's too bad. I never thought that he'd become a **dropout.**

6. **féel frée to** = don't hesitate to

S1: It was so nice to see you. I hope we'll be able to get together again soon.
S2: **Feel free to** call me any time.

7. **kéep in tóuch/stáy in tóuch (with)** = stay in contact with ≠ **lóse tóuch**

S1: It was good talking to you.
S2: (Let's) **keep/stay in touch** (with each other).
S1: I agree. Let's not **lose touch.**

Similar expressions:

>**be in tóuch (with)** ≠ **be óut of tóuch (with)**

S1: Are you **in touch with** Steve?
S2: No, we've been **out of touch** for two years.

>**gét báck in tóuch (with)** = **gét in tóuch** again

S1: I thought you two **lost touch.**
S2: We did, but we **got back in touch** when we saw each other at Dorothy's party.

8. rún ínto *(inseparable/transitive)* = meet unexpectedly = **búmp ínto**

S1: I **ran into** our old English teacher in the supermarket. I couldn't believe it.
S2: I'll bet you never expected to **run into** her!

Contrast:

S1: Look! That crazy driver **ran into** (= crashed into) a tree.
S2: Stop at that phone so we can call an ambulance.

■ Exercises

1. Mini-Dialogues

Below are two columns, A and B. Column A contains the first lines of dialogues and column B contains possible responses. For each opening line in column A, choose the *best* response from column B.

When checking this exercise in class, perform each mini-dialogue. One student should read an item from column A, and another student should respond with the answer from column B.

	A		B
_____ **1.**	Why don't you stay for a while?	**a.**	Let me help you move them out of the way.
_____ **2.**	I hate to say good-bye, but it's time to board the plane.	**b.**	Because I'm late for work.
_____ **3.**	Thanks for dropping in.	**c.**	No problem. You're on my way.
_____ **4.**	I can't make a speech in front of the whole class!	**d.**	Let's go. It feels like we've been here for ages.
_____ **5.**	Did you see what happened?	**e.**	No, I haven't seen her in ages.
_____ **6.**	Why are you in a hurry?	**f.**	No, because people were in my way.
_____ **7.**	I have to set the table for dinner, but the table is full of books.	**g.**	Do we have to? It's out of our way and we'll be late.
_____ **8.**	I saw my old girlfriend at the cafe.	**h.**	Remember to keep in touch.
_____ **9.**	This movie is terrible. It's so long and boring.	**i.**	Did you run into her, or did you plan to meet?
_____ **10.**	Have you seen Margaret lately?	**j.**	I wish I could, but I have an appointment so I have to get going.
_____ **11.**	Can you give me a ride home?	**k.**	It was great talking to you.
_____ **12.**	I have to stop at the bank.	**l.**	Come on. You can do it!

2. Choosing the Idiom

The following dialogue takes place between the man and woman in the illustration. Fill in the blanks with some of the expressions on the list. Pay special attention to how the expressions are used grammatically. (You will need to consider verb tenses, subject-verb agreement, plurals, etc.) After you have checked your answers, perform the dialogue with a partner.

come on	out of touch
drop in	out of the way
drop in at	in the way
in ages	get going
for ages	feel free to
run into	

LIZ: Dick!

DICK: Liz! I never thought I'd _____ you here!
        (1)

        I haven't seen you _____ .How are you?
        (2)

LIZ: Not bad. How about you?

DICK: Fine. What's new?

LIZ: Nothing special.

DICK: I knew I would see you again sometime, somewhere. Let's pay for our

groceries and go get some coffee.

LIZ: Sorry, I can't.

DICK: _____ (3) . You can find five minutes for me.

LIZ: Listen, I have to _____ (4) . Please move your

shopping cart _____ (5) so I can do my shopping.

DICK: Can I _____ (6) some time so that we can talk? I

don't like being _____ (7) with you.

LIZ: I'm really busy.

DICK: Well then, _____ (8) call me any time. You know

the number. It was great seeing you.

3. Dictation

Your teacher or one of your classmates will read the dictation for this unit from Appendix A, or you will listen to the dictation on the audio program. You will hear the dictation three times. First, just listen. Second, as you listen, write the dictation on a separate sheet of paper. Third, as you listen, check what you have written.

4. Any Questions?

Take out a piece of paper. Do NOT write your name on it. On one side of the paper, write down what you think is the most interesting information that you have learned in this lesson up to now. On the other side of the paper, write down any questions that you have about any of the idioms. Your teacher will collect this paper and then answer your questions the next time you meet.

5. Personal Questions

Answer the questions below in a conversation with a partner or small group.

1. What is something that you haven't done in ages that you would like to do again?

2. What is something that you have been doing for ages that you would like to stop doing?

3. Describe a situation in which someone was in your way. Where were you? About how old was the other person? What did you do or say and how did the other person react?

4. Explain what happened the last time you dropped in on someone or someone dropped in on you.

5. Have you ever lost touch with someone that you really liked? If yes, what happened?

6. How often and where do you run into people that you know in your community?

6. Skit Writing

In this illustration, Judy and Brian run into each other while jogging. They haven't seen each other since they graduated from high school six years ago. In high school they always liked each other, but they never were boyfriend and girlfriend.

Work individually, in pairs, or as a class to write their conversation. Try to use at least five new expressions from this lesson, and at least one expression from Lesson One. After you have finished, perform the "skit" you created for your class.

7. Improvisation

Using the new expressions from this lesson, act out the following role-play. The new expressions should be written on the board.

You and your boyfriend or girlfriend (or husband or wife) are at a party for graduates of a school that you once attended. You see people that you knew many years ago. With your partner, find out who has gotten married, who has gotten divorced, who has had children, who went to college, and where your old classmates now work. Remember to introduce your partner to your old friends.

Possible starting lines:
Jon! Remember me? I'm . . .

or

Ruth? Is that you? I . . .

8. Real Life

Think of situations in your own life in which you might use some of the expressions from this lesson. Write down at least five. Outside of class, remember your list and try to use some of your new vocabulary. Also, when you watch TV and listen to people speak, listen carefully—you may hear these expressions.

Expressions	*Real-Life Situations*
Example: *in my way*	*in a movie theater, telling my friend that I can't see because someone's head is in my way*
1.	
2.	
3.	
4.	
5.	

Please Leave a Message After You Hear the Beep

TELEPHONE RECORDING: This is 510-2878. **Please leave a message after you hear the beep.**

MELISSA (thinking): Oh, no. I can't do it . . . Everyone has an answering machine these days. It's really **a pain.** I'm going to **go out of my mind.** I'm going to **hang up** . . . but I have to **leave a message.** I know, I'll **write it down** so I can **call back** and read it . . . Where's a pencil? . . . OK . . . I'll say, "Hi, **this is** Melissa. I'm calling about the apartment for rent. Please call me back at 415-2550. I'm usually here in the evening. Thank you." OK . . . Where's that number?

STEVE: Melissa—What's **going on?** You look so nervous. Can you **stand still** for a minute?

MELISSA: No, I can't. I'm trying to **get up the nerve to** leave a message on someone's answering machine.

STEVE: You're afraid of answering machines?

MELISSA: Uh-huh. I **freeze** and **get tongue-tied,** and I don't really know why. I just don't like talking into a machine.

STEVE: Want me to do it for you?

MELISSA: Thanks, but I think I should do this **on my own.** I wrote down what I want to say and I **was just about ready to** call and leave a message when you walked in.

STEVE: **Good for you.** Do you want me to leave while you **make your call?**

MELISSA: **Don't be silly.** Just **have a seat** and **wish me luck!** OK now . . . I'd better **take a deep breath** first . . . all right . . . **here goes!**

QUESTIONS
1. Why is Melissa so nervous?
2. How do you feel when you speak into an answering machine?
3. Are answering machines commonly used in your native country?

■ Understanding the New Expressions

1. Pléase léave a méssage áfter (you héar) the béep.

S1: You have reached 209-1764. No one can come to the phone right now. **Please leave a message after the beep** and we'll call you back. *(beep)*

S2: Hi Russ. Want to have lunch at 12? Leave a message on my machine to let me know. I'll be **checking my messages.**

Similar expression: **Pléase léave a méssage áfter the tóne.**

Related expression: **chéck one's méssages**—*It is possible with many answering machines to find out if you have any messages even if you are not near your machine. To "check your messages," you call your own phone number and then press special numbers on a touch-tone phone.*

2. a páin = something or someone that is annoying or troublesome

S1: Writing letters is **a pain** for me. I'd rather call someone.
S2: I'm exactly the opposite. I'd much rather write than call.

Similar expression: **a páin in the néck**

Lesson 3

—Leaving messages on answering machines is **a pain in the neck** for me.
—Writing letters is **a pain in the neck** for me.
—They are really **a pain in the neck.** They always want something from us.

3. **gó óut of one's mínd** = go crazy

S1: I have so much to do that I'm **going out of my mind.**
S2: Maybe you need to take a break.

Similar expression: **be óut of one's mínd** = *be* crazy

—You**'re out of your mind!** Why are you driving so fast in this traffic?
—They **are out of their minds.** How can they ride their bikes at night without lights?

Note: *First people "go" out of their minds, and then they "are" out of their minds.*

Note: *A typical gesture that indicates that someone thinks a person is crazy involves pointing the index finger at the side of the head and turning the finger in a circular motion.*

Similar, but very informal expressions:

> **be/gó núts**
> **be/gó banánas**
> **be/gó óff one's rócker**

4. **háng úp** (separable, transitive) = put a telephone receiver down to turn off a phone

S1: I'm sorry. I need to **hang up** right now because someone's at my door.
S2: OK. I'll talk to you at school.

Related expression: **háng úp on (*someone*)** = be so angry when talking on the phone that you end the conversation without saying good-bye—you just hang up

S1: I don't believe you at all!
S2: That's O.K. with me! (Speaker 2 **hangs up on** Speaker 1 without saying good-bye.)

Other telephone expressions:

> When the phone rings and someone is there, that person **answers** the phone. If no one is there, the caller can say. **"There's no answer."**
> When you **make a call** (or **call** someone), you identify yourself by saying, **"This is ____."** (not "I am ____.")
> When you answer the phone and the caller asks to speak with someone else, such as your sister, you tell your sister, **"It's Adam."**
> When you are talking, you are ***on the phone.***

If you are talking on the phone, but need to stop the conversation for a minute, you can ask the other person to **hold on,** or to **hold.**

Businesses often ask callers if they can **put you on hold,** or if you can **hold.**

If you are home but you don't want to answer the phone, and you have an answering machine, you can let the answering machine answer the phone. In this situation, you **screen your calls.**

If the person you are calling is not there, you can say, "Can I **leave a message?**" Or, the person you are talking to can ask you, "Would you like to **leave a message?**" or "Can I **take a message?**"

If the person you are calling is not there, and an answering machine answers your call, you can **leave a message** on **the machine.**

If you leave a message, you might say that you will **call back** (call again) later. Or, you might ask if the person you want to talk to can **call you back** later.

If the person you are calling is already on the phone, you will hear a **busy signal.** This means that **the line is busy.**

Some people have **call waiting.** If you have call waiting, when you are talking on the phone and someone else is trying to call you, you will hear a sound. You can say to the person you are talking to, **"Sorry. I have another call. Can you hold (on) for a minute?"** Then you can press a button, talk to the other person, press the button again, and be back to the first person you were talking to. Many people don't like this system because it interrupts the first conversation.

5. **write** *something* **down** (separable/transitive) = write on a piece of paper

S1: My phone number is 642-5933. Can you remember that?
S2: Probably not. I'd better **write** it **down.** Do you have a pen?

Note: *To "write" something is not exactly the same. You write a letter, but you don't write down a letter. You write down specific information such as phone numbers, addresses, notes, etc., in order to remember it.*

6. be **going on** = be happening

S1: What's **going on** in here? Who are all these people?
S2: Oh, hi, Dad. We're having a party. I hope it's OK . . .

S1: What's new?
S2: Oh, there's so much **going on.** My sister just had a baby, our dog ran away, we're going to move . . .

Note: *This expression is usually used in the present continuous tense.*

7. **stánd still** = not move

S1: Uh-oh—you'd better **stand still.** There's a bee on your shirt.
S2: Oh no! Get it off!

S1: Listen, I'll fix your hair if you'll just **stand still.**
S2: I am **standing still.**
S1: No, you aren't. You keep moving and I can't do this.

8. **gét up the nérve (to dó** *something***)** = get the courage to do something

S1: I want to ask her to marry me, but I can't **get up the nerve** to ask.
S2: Are you afraid that she'll say no?

S1: I've been working there for two years without a raise, and I need to **get up the nerve to** talk to my boss.
S2: You really should. Do you want to practice on me?

9. **fréeze** = get so scared that you can't move

S1: When I got to the front of the class to make my speech, I **froze** and forgot everything I was going to say.
S2: Then what hapened?
S1: My teacher reminded me to use my notes.

10. **gét tóngue-tied** = become so nervous that you are unable to talk

S1: I always **get tongue-tied** when I talk to people who have power.
S2: What do you mean?
S1: Oh, you know, people like teachers and bosses. They make me so nervous that I can't talk.

Similar expression: **be tóngue-tied** = be unable to talk because of being very nervous

S1: Come on. Tell me what happened.
S2: Uh . . . I . . .
S1: What happened? Are you **tongue-tied** all of a sudden?

11. dó *something* ón one's ówn = do something alone, without help

> **S1:** Mom, I need help with my math homework. I don't understand this.
> **S2:** You're already 22 years old! You should be able to do your homework **on your own** by now.
>
> **S1:** Let me help you.
> **S2:** No, thanks. I'd rather do it **on my own.**

> *Similar expression:* dó *something* (by) onesélf = do something on one's own

> **S1:** Let me help you.
> **S2:** No, thanks. I'd rather **do it (by) myself.**
>
> **S1:** Why don't you help him?
> **S2:** I offered to help, but he said he wanted to **do it by himself.**

12. be (júst) about (réady) to dó *something* = be almost ready to do something

> **S1:** Hello?
> **S2:** Irene? Hi! This is Nicole. You sound like you're in a hurry.
> **S1:** I'm sorry, I am. I **was just about (ready) to leave.** Can I call you back tonight?
> **S2:** Sure. I'll be home around seven.

13. Góod for yóu! = That's great—you plan to do something good or you have already succeeded in doing something

> **S1:** I'm going to get a job working with disabled children.
> **S2:** **Good for you!**
>
> **S1:** I got an A on my test!/I got the job!/I finished my homework.
> **S2:** **Good for you!**

14. Dón't be sílly! = Don't be ridiculous!
> Don't do or say something that doesn't make sense.

> **S1:** Come on. I'll be glad to drive you home.
> **S2:** But it's so far.
> **S1:** **Don't be silly!** It's not that far. Let's go.

15. Háve a séat. = This is a friendly and polite way to ask someone to sit down.

> **S1:** Come on in and **have a seat.** I'll be right with you.
> **S2:** Thanks.

16. Wísh me lúck! = You can say this to someone as you are about to start something new.

> **S1:** You'd better get going now. Your interview is in an hour, isn't it?
> **S2:** Yeah, you're right. **Wish me luck!**
> **S1:** Good luck. Don't worry. You'll get the job. Just be yourself.

17. **táke a déep bréath** = breathe deeply, either to relax or so your doctor can hear your lungs

S1: You're next. **Take a deep breath,** and then go to the front of the class.
S2: I'm really nervous.

—(Doctor:) **Take a deep breath** and then breathe out slowly.

Note: *Remember that "breath" is a noun and that "breathe" is a verb. We "breathe" air all the time; we should "take a deep breath" when we're nervous.*

Other expressions with "breath":

be óut of bréath = breathe fast after running or going up a lot of stairs
have bád bréath = have breath that doesn't smell good because you either didn't brush your teeth or you ate some food that left an odor

18. **Hére góes!** = This is something someone might say about one second before starting something that's a little scary.

S1: Do you really expect me to jump out of this airplane?
S2: Sure. You've got your parachute on and we've talked all about it. Well?
S1: You're right. OK. **Here goes!** (Ahhhhhhhhhhhhhhh!)

S1: This water is so cold!
S2: No, it isn't. Just jump in and you'll be OK.
S1: All right. You'd better be right. **Here goes!** . . . God! It's freezing!

1. Mini-Dialogues

Below are two columns, A and B. Column A contains the first lines of dialogues and column B contains possible responses. For each opening line in column A, choose the *best* response from column B.

When checking this exercise in class, perform each mini-dialogue. One student should read an item from column A and another student should respond with the answer from column B.

<table>
<tr><td colspan="2" align="center">A</td><td align="center">B</td></tr>
<tr><td>____</td><td>1. Have a seat. I'll be right with you.</td><td>a. I'd better write that down.</td></tr>
<tr><td>____</td><td>2. I'm going to write an article for the school newspaper about the educational system in my native country.</td><td>b. Do you think you can find one?</td></tr>
<tr><td>____</td><td>3. What's going on in here? Why are the lights out?</td><td>c. Hi, Joni? This is Jean. Can you call me back? Thanks.</td></tr>
<tr><td>____</td><td>4. Oh, I have another call. Can you hold on for a minute?</td><td>d. Thanks, but I should try to do it on my own.</td></tr>
<tr><td>____</td><td>5. The homework for tomorrow is on pages 36, 42, 45, 46, 49, and 50.</td><td>e. Thanks.</td></tr>
<tr><td>____</td><td>6. Please leave a message after you hear the beep.</td><td>f. I did, but his line was busy.</td></tr>
<tr><td>____</td><td>7. Didn't you call Larry?</td><td>g. She must have been really embarrassed.</td></tr>
<tr><td>____</td><td>8. This traffic is a real pain in the neck. I'm going to get a job closer to home.</td><td>h. Then you should use your video camera instead.</td></tr>
<tr><td>____</td><td>9. If you don't stand still, I won't be able to take your picture.</td><td>i. Good for you!</td></tr>
<tr><td>____</td><td>10. I was just about to go to bed when the phone rang and I got the news.</td><td>j. I bet you had trouble falling asleep.</td></tr>
<tr><td>____</td><td>11. Your whole family can stay in my house.</td><td>k. Surprise! Happy Birthday!</td></tr>
<tr><td>____</td><td>12. Let me help you.</td><td>l. Don't be silly! You don't have enough room.</td></tr>
<tr><td>____</td><td>13. How did you get up the nerve to say that?</td><td>m. Well, first I took a deep breath, and then I looked him in the eye and told him.</td></tr>
<tr><td>____</td><td>14. When the teacher asked her why she copied her friend's homework, she was tongue-tied.</td><td>n. Only for a minute. I'm in a hurry.</td></tr>
</table>

2. Choosing the Idiom

The following dialogue takes place between the person in the illustration and a telephone operator. Fill in the blanks with some of the expressions on the list. Pay special attention to how the expressions are used grammatically. (You will need to consider verb tenses, subject-verb agreement, plurals, etc.) After you have checked your answers, perform the dialogue with a partner.

a busy signal	call back	go out of one's mind
leave a message	be just about ready	a pain in the neck
going on	hang up	Sorry, I have another call. Can you hold on?

TELEPHONE RECORDING: Thank you for calling. If you have a touch-tone phone and would like information about your phone bill, press 1 now. If you would like to change your service or arrange new telephone service, press 2 now. If you would like information about our telephone store, press 3 now. If you have a rotary phone, please stay on the line and an operator will help you shortly.

MELISSA: I _____ ! Every time I pick up a phone, I
(1)

hear a machine. I guess I should press 2 . . . Boy, they really play terrible

music while they make you wait.

(5 minutes later)

MELISSA: What's _____ (2) _____ here? I've been waiting at

least five minutes. I'll have to _____ (3) _____ later

. . . Hello? Oh, I _____ (4) _____ to _____ (5) _____ .

OPERATOR: Sorry to keep you waiting. How may I help you?

MELISSA: Hi. I'd like to cancel my "call waiting" service.

OPERATOR: May I have your number please?

MELISSA: 415-2550.

OPERATOR: OK. We can put that change into effect starting tomorrow morning. May

I ask your reason for canceling this service?

MELISSA: Sure. My friends don't like the interruption. They say they would rather

hear _____ (6) _____ than hear me say,

" _____ (7) _____ .

_____ (8) _____ ?" To be honest with you, I don't

like the interruption either.

3. Dictation

Your teacher or one of your classmates will read the dictation for this unit from Appendix A, or you will listen to the dictation on the audio program. You will hear the dictation three times. First, just listen. Second, as you listen, write the dictation on a separate sheet of paper. Third, as you listen, check what you have written.

4. Any Questions?

Take out a piece of paper. Do NOT write your name on it. On one side of the paper, write down what you think is the most interesting information that you have learned in this lesson up to now. On the other side of the paper, write down any questions that you have about any of the idioms. Your teacher will collect this paper and then answer your questions the next time you meet.

5. Personal Questions

Answer the questions below in a conversation with a partner or in a small group.

1. Do you have an answering machine? If yes, do you like having it? Do you ever "screen" calls? Tell the others what your greeting says.
   If you don't have an answering machine, would you like to get one some day? Why or why not? If you had a machine, what would your greeting be?

2. What do you do when you call a person or place that has an answering machine and you have to speak English? Do you ever hang up and write down what you want to say?

3. Do you ever prefer to talk to a machine to save time? In other words, have you ever called someone when you knew they wouldn't be home because it would be faster to leave a quick message than have a conversation?

4. Have you ever heard of "telephone tag"? It's an expression that means that, for example, you leave a message on a friend's machine. When your friend returns your call, he or she leaves a message on your machine. Basically, you communicate through your machines rather than personally. What do you think of this?

5. Do you have "call waiting"? If yes, do you like it? Why or why not?

6. Have you ever been talking to someone who has "call waiting" and been interrupted by another call? If yes, how did you feel?

7. The telephone recording in Exercise 2 is an example of what voice mail can say. Some people get very upset with this because you keep pressing numbers and may have trouble finding a real person to talk to. Have you ever called a place that uses voice mail? If yes, what did you do? Did you get the information that you wanted?

8. Have you ever seen people talking on cellular phones while driving? If yes, what do you think of this?

9. How common are answering machines, call waiting, voice mail, and cellular phones in your native country?

10. Find out what a *beeper* and a *fax machine* are, if you don't already know. How common are these in your native country?

11. Consider all of the modern innovations that you have just discussed. In general, do you think the world is better or worse because of them? Explain.

6. Skit Writing

In the first illustration, Norm is leaving a message on Alice's answering machine. He's sorry she isn't home because he needs to talk to her about how nervous he is about making a speech in class tomorrow.

In the second illustration, Alice returns Norm's call. Norm explains that when he is in front of a group of people, he freezes. But he wants to try. Alice gives him encouragement.

Work individually, in pairs, or as a class to write their conversation. Try to use at least five new expressions from this lesson and two expressions from previous lessons. After you have finished, perform the "skit" you created for your class.

7. Improvisation

Using the new expressions from this lesson, act out the following role-play. The new expressions should be written on the board.

You are asleep, having a nightmare. You are dreaming that you are calling all of your classmates to find out what the homework is, and everyone you are calling has an answering machine. And each person has a different greeting. You feel like you are going out of your mind, but you keep making phone calls. Between the calls you talk to yourself.

(One greeting can be an imitation of voice mail—for example—"Press 1 if you want to know how I am; Press 2 if you want to know what the homework is," etc.)

Possible starting lines:
Oh, no! Not another answering machine!

8. Real Life

Think of situations in your own life in which you might use some of the expressions from this lesson. Write down at least five. Outside of class, remember your list and try to use some of your new vocabulary. Also, when you watch TV and listen to people speak, listen carefully—you may hear these expressions.

Expressions	*Real-Life Situations*
Example: *a pain in the neck*	*I say this when I talk about my little sister when she wants my attention and I'm busy*
1.	
2.	
3.	
4.	
5.	

Lesson

In Bad Shape

CARMEN: Hello?

NICK: Carmen? Is that you? Are you OK?

CARMEN: Uh-uh, I **caught a** terrible **cold.**

NICK: You too? Well, **I have news for you.** We're **in the same boat!** Ahchoo!

CARMEN: Bless you.

NICK: Thanks.

CARMEN: Why don't you come over and **keep me company?** I haven't talked to anyone **all day long.**

NICK: I'd like to, but I **can't stop** sneezing. Ahchoo! Ahchoo! And I have a sore throat. I just want to go to bed.

CARMEN: **I know what you mean.** Do you have a fever?

NICK: I don't know for sure, but I think so. I was going to **take my temperature,** but I dropped the thermometer and it broke.

CARMEN: **It sounds like** you should just . . . ahchoo! Excuse me. You should just take two aspirin and go to bed. **Chances are** you'll feel better in the morning.

NICK: I hope so. And I hope you'll **get over** your cold soon. Are you going to school tomorrow?

CARMEN: I don't think so. **I'm in** really **bad shape.** I may have to be absent for a few more days.

NICK: Listen to us! We **feel sorry for** ourselves today, don't we?

QUESTIONS
1. What do you say when someone sneezes or coughs?
2. When you have a cold, what do you do? Do you take medicine? If yes, what kind? What food do you eat, and what do you drink?
3. To convert Fahrenheit to centigrade, use the formula $C = F - 32 \times (5 \div 9)$. To convert centigrade to Fahrenheit, use the formula $F = C \times (9 \div 5) + 32$. The normal body temperature on the centigrade scale is 37°. What is the normal body temperature on the Fahrenheit scale?

■ Understanding the New Expressions

1. cátch a cóld/háve a cóld (PAST = caught)
cátch the flú/háve the flú

S1: You'd better not come near me. I have a terrible sore throat, and I can't stop sneezing.
S2: You **caught** another **cold?** I hope you don't **have the flu.**

2. **I have néws for you.** (Or: **I've got néws for you.**) = I have something to tell you.

   S1: He just told me that I won't be able to work here any more.
   S2: **I have news for you.** He just told the same thing to twenty other people.

3. **be in the sáme bóat** = be in the same unpleasant situation

   S1: I'll have to stay up all night to study for that exam.
   S2: **I'm in the same boat!** I'll have to stay up, too.
   S1: Why don't we study together?

   S1: I can't believe that we got a flat tire.
   S2: Look across the street. Those people **are in the same boat!**

4. **kéep *someone* cómpany** = stay with someone who doesn't want to be alone

   S1: I have to go now.
   S2: Please don't go yet. **Keep me company** for just a little while.

   S1: Are you going alone? Do you want someone to **keep you company?**
   S2: Sure! That would be great!

5. **áll dáy (lóng)/áll níght (lóng)**

   S1: My eyes hurt.
   S2: I'm not surprised. You've been reading that book **all day long.**

6. **cán't stóp** (+ *gerund*) = be unable to stop a habit or an activity

   S1: What am I going to do? I **can't stop smoking.**
   S2: If you really wanted to, you would.

   Contrast: **cán't stóp to** (+ *base form of verb*) = be unable to stop an activity so you can do something else

   S1: Can you stop writing for a while? I want to discuss something with you.
   S2: I **can't stop to talk** now. I have to finish this report.

7. **I knów what you méan.**

   S1: He's always telling people what to do.
   S2: **I know what you mean.** My uncle is like that.

   Similar expressions:

   What do you méan?

   S1: He's very bossy.
   S2: **What do you mean?**
   S1: Well, he's always telling people what to do.

S1: He's very bossy.
S2: **What does that mean?**
S1: Bossy? It means that he acts like a boss. He's always telling people what to do.

8. **táke** *someone's* **témperature** = use a thermometer to find out if someone has a fever

S1: Her forehead seems warm.
S2: Let's get the thermometer and **take** her **temperature.**

Related expression: have a fever, have fever

S1: Her temperature is 101°F (38.3°C).
S2: Well, normal is only 98.6°F (37°C). She **has a fever.** (or: She **has fever.**)
S1: Let's call the doctor.

9. **sóund(s) like** (+ *noun phrase*)
   sound(s) + *adjective*

S1: I have three exams next week.
S2: It **sounds like** school is keeping you busy.

S1: Have you seen any reviews of that new movie?
S2: Yes, I've seen a few. It **sounds** great.

Contrast: **sóund(s)** *(literal)*

S1: Have you heard Mike play his violin?
S2: Yes, I have. He **sounds** awful.
S1: Well, he's had only one lesson.

10. **chánces are** = probably

S1: Where's Gary?
S2: He was sneezing a lot last night. **Chances are** he's staying home today.

11. **gét óver** (*something or someone*) (inseparable/transitive) = recover from

S1: I have an important appointment next week. I'd better **get over** this cold by then.
S2: Well, don't go back to work until you're feeling better.

S1: Carol's boyfriend left her two months ago, and she still hasn't **gotten over** him.
S2: Let's introduce her to Jerry. She might like him.

12. **be in góod shápe** ≠ **be in bád shápe** = be in good or bad physical condition

S1: How are you doing?
S2: I'**m in bad shape.** I have a sore throat and a high fever.

S1: You look like you'**re in** really **good shape**!
S2: Thanks. I've been exercising.

Contrast: These expressions can also have a psychological meaning:

S1: How are you doing?
S2: I'**m in** pretty **good shape.** No big problems. And you?

S1: How are you doing?
S2: I'**m in bad shape.** I have two books to read for school and I haven't even started them.

13. **féel sórry for** (*someone*)

S1: Why did you give that guy a dollar?
S2: I **feel sorry for** him.

S1: Look at him. His girlfriend left him and now he **feels sorry for** himself.
S2: He'll get over her soon.

Note: It is not polite to directly tell another person, 'I feel sorry for you.'"

1. Mini-Dialogues

Below are two columns, A and B. Column A contains the first lines of dialogues and column B contains possible responses. For each opening line in column A, choose the *best* response from column B.

When checking this exercise in class, perform each mini-dialogue. One student should read an item from column A and another student should respond with the answer from column B.

A	B
_____ **1.** Bless you!	**a.** I know, but I can't stop to eat until I finish what I'm doing.
_____ **2.** Amy! I haven't seen you in a long time! Have you been sick?	**b.** I know, but I'll never get over him.
_____ **3.** I'd better hurry so I can catch the 11 o'clock bus.	**c.** Mmm. It's delicious. I can't stop eating.
_____ **4.** I missed my flight and can't get another one 'til 2 a.m.	**d.** It sounds like they had a good time.
_____ **5.** You were in a car accident, weren't you?	**e.** I know what you mean. I have the same problem.
_____ **6.** Ron is staying with you? That's nice.	**f.** Thanks. I guess I caught a cold.
_____ **7.** Did you have a good time?	**g.** Yes, he's keeping me company while my roommate is away.
_____ **8.** Do you like the dinner?	**h.** Uh-huh. I had the flu, but I'm OK now.
_____ **9.** Let's take a break and have lunch. You've been working all morning.	**i.** Uh-huh. But don't worry. I'm in good shape now.
_____ **10.** It's hard to say the English "th" sound because you have to put your tongue between your teeth.	**j.** It was great. We laughed all night long.
_____ **11.** He has a high fever.	**k.** No I don't. I got over it.
_____ **12.** Do you know when she'll be home?	**l.** I have news for you. It's already 11:30.
_____ **13.** They had dinner out, and then they went to a movie.	**m.** Maybe he should go to the doctor.
_____ **14.** What a movie! People were killing each other for two hours.	**n.** You know, I'm in the same boat. Why don't we go into the city for a few hours?
_____ **15.** Do you want to go to the zoo?	**o.** She said around 9, so chances are she'll be here soon.
_____ **16.** Forget about Jeff. There are lots of other men in the world.	**p.** It sounds terrible.
	q. Not really. I always feel so sorry for those poor animals in cages.

2. Choosing the Idiom

The following dialogue takes place between the two people in the illustration. Fill in the blanks with some of the expressions on the list. Pay special attention to how the expressions are used grammatically. (You will need to consider verb tenses, subject-verb agreement, plurals, etc.) After you have checked your answers, perform the dialogue with a partner.

catch/have a cold
catch/have the flu
I have news for you
be in the same boat
keep (someone) company
all day long
all night long
can't stop
feel sorry for
be in good/bad shape

What do you mean
What does that mean
Do you know what I mean
I know what you mean
take (someone's) temperature
sound like
chances are
get over

VET: So, what seems to be the problem?

MAN: Tuck was awake _____(1)_____ . And this morning he

wouldn't eat anything. And look, he _____(2)_____

pulling on his right ear.

VET: It _____(3)_____ something is wrong. Will you help me

Lesson 4

hold him so I can _____ (4) _____ ? Thanks. . . . Yes, he

does have a fever.

MAN: I _____ (5) _____ him. Look at his sad eyes.

VET: _____ (6) _____ he'll be better by tomorrow. These pills

will help him _____ (7) _____ his infection quickly.

MAN: What infection?

VET: He has an ear infection.

MAN: Really? We _____ (8) _____ . I have an ear infection too!

VET: That is a coincidence. But you look like you

_____ (9) _____ .

MAN: I'm better now because I've been taking medicine.

VET: And that's exactly what Tuck will do. You can pick him up tomorrow.

MAN: _____ (10) _____ ?

VET: I mean that I'd like to keep him here overnight.

MAN: But I live alone! I need him to _____ (11) _____ .

VET: It's only for one night.

MAN: _____ (12) _____ . One night is a long time. Tuck is coming

home with me!

3. Dictation

Your teacher or one of your classmates will read the dictation for this unit from Appendix A, or you will listen to the dictation on the audio program. You will hear the dictation three times. First, just listen. Second, as you listen, write the dictation on a separate sheet of paper. Third, as you listen, check what you have written.

4. Any Questions?

Take out a piece of paper. Do NOT write your name on it. On one side of the paper, write down what you think is the most interesting information that you have learned in this lesson up to now. On the other side of the paper, write down any questions that you have about any of the idioms. Your teacher will collect this paper and then answer your questions the next time you meet.

5. Personal Questions

Answer the questions below in a conversation with a partner or in a small group.

1. How do you act when you have a cold or the flu? Do you complain a lot? Are you happy to stay home from school or work? Do you expect your family or someone else to take care of you?

2. When you have a cold or a stomach virus, what medical treatment(s) do you use? What do you eat or drink? Are these treatments used in your native country?

3. "Hypochondriacs" are people who think they are sick, but they are not. They say things like:

> My head hurts.
> I feel rotten (terrible).
> Oh, my stomach is killing me.
> Please wash the dishes because I don't feel well.

Do you know any hypochondriacs? If yes, who are they and what do they say?

4. Ask your partner or group members about language problems they are having, and decide in which areas you are "in the same boat."

5. Do you feel sorry for anyone you know? If yes, who and why?

6. In what situations do you like to have someone keep you company?

6. Skit Writing

In this illustration, the astronaut is being examined by his doctor. The astronaut is scheduled to go on a flight into outer space tomorrow, but the doctor informs him that he has a cold and will not be able to go. The astronaut is very disappointed.

Work individually, in pairs, or as a class to write their conversation. Try to use at least five new expressions from this lesson and two expressions from previous lessons. After you have finished, perform the "skit" you created for your class.

7. Improvisation

Using the new expressions from this lesson, act out the following role-play. The new expressions should be written on the board.

You are scheduled to represent your country in the Summer Olympics. You are planning to be in the swimming race the next day, but you are sneezing and coughing and have a headache. You talk to two other swimmers from other countries and find out that they have the same problem.

Possible starting line:
Ahchoo . . . Ahchoo . . . Excuse me . . . Do you have a tissue?

8. Real Life

Think of situations in your own life in which you might use some of the expressions from this lesson. Write down at least five. Outside of class, remember your list and try to use some of your new vocabulary. Also, when you watch TV and listen to people speak, listen carefully—you may hear these expressions.

Expressions	*Real-Life Situations*
Example: *be in good shape*	*I would look at the people doing exercises at a health spa and think about which ones are in good shape.*
1.	
2.	
3.	
4.	
5.	

Crossword Puzzle

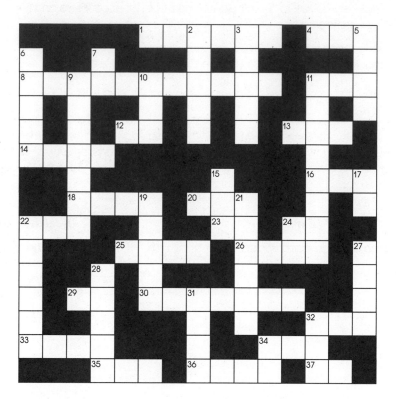

Across

1. I'm having _____ thoughts about buying that new car.

4. Can you drop me _____ at the corner?

8. I need to take my _____ . Where is the thermometer?

11. I love you. Let's _____ the knot.

12. Write. Let's keep _____ touch.

13. They feel sorry _____ homeless animals.

14. Let's never _____ touch.

16. He _____ up the nerve to ask her to lend him some money.

18. She _____ bananas every time she hears that song.

20. He is _____ of his mind.

22. They aren't single—they _____ married.

23. I was just about ready _____ leave when you called.

24. Why don't you drop in _____ my house later?

25. I have a lot of work, too. We're in the same _____ .

26. They're going _____ with all their homework.

29. I need to check _____ messages. I'll be right back.

30. I'll call you when we're _____ with dinner.

32. We've been waiting _____ ages. Maybe we should call.

33. I'd better write that _____ before I forget.
34. They've been laughing _____ night long.
35. Let's _____ married as soon as possible.
36. _____ be silly! You can do it.
37. I'm sorry. I have to hang _____ now because someone else needs the phone.

Down

2. I don't want to _____ a cold.
3. He's trying to get up the _____ to ask her for a date.
5. We have cold _____ about going there.
6. Stand _____ . You keep moving.
7. You'll probably wind _____ rich.
9. Please leave a _____ after the tone.
10. Every time I go to the store, I _____ into someone I know.
11. They are having second _____ about buying a house.
15. _____ that out! You're bothering me!
17. I'm dying _____ see that movie.
19. Can I ask you something? Sure! _____ !
21. He couldn't talk—he was _____ -tied.
22. Everything is so expensive here. I can't even _____ coffee.
24. same as 24 across
27. I hope I get _____ this cold before my job interview.
28. He's _____ of thirst. Is there any water here?
31. My mother knows what I'm thinking. She can _____ my mind.
32. She's absent because she has the _____ .
34. same as 24 down

Tic Tac Toe

In this variation of tic tac toe, to get an X or an O you must create a grammatically correct sentence that is logical in meaning. Here is a game to start you off. Create as many games as you like, using expressions from Lessons 1–4.

get up the nerve to	feel sorry for	be in good shape
be in the same boat	read someone's mind	I have news for you...
Stand still	run into	wind up

Guess the Idiom

Look at these cartoons and try to guess which expressions from Lessons 1–4 they represent.

1. _____

2. _____

3. _____

4. _____

5. _____

6. _____

Are We Couch Potatoes?

ANDY: Hi guys. Come on in. You didn't have to bring anything.

SUSAN: We know that, but we wanted to. I'm so glad we could finally **get together.**

RUTH: Let me take your coats. Come in and **make yourselves comfortable.** How are you doing tonight?

MICHAEL: Pretty good. We rented two old movies. What **are you in the mood to** see first—the **tearjerker** or the horror movie?

RUTH: **How about** the horror movie first? I don't **feel like crying** right now. I'd rather **be scared out of my wits,** if I have a choice.

MICHAEL: **That makes two of us.**

(DURING THE MOVIE)

ANDY: Maybe we should turn a light on. This movie is getting a little scary.

RUTH: Andy!

ANDY: I **was just kidding.** Could you **move over** a little? It's getting kind of crowded here.

SUSAN: I'll sit on the floor.

ANDY: No . . .

SUSAN: Really . . . I want to. Could you pass the popcorn please?

MICHAEL: **Here you go.** Who has the remote control? Can you **hit pause?** Thanks . . . I have a question . . . Do you think we're **couch potatoes?**

ANDY: **Why do you ask?**

MICHAEL: Well, we do **spend a lot of time** sitting on the couch, **glued to the tube** and eating snacks. Sometimes I think I've become **a couch potato.**

SUSAN: **That's funny,** Michael. I thought you **were a bookworm** because you read so much. It's hard to get you to **put a book down.**

MICHAEL: I think I'm watching TV more and reading less . . .

ANDY: Can we talk about this later? **I'm** really **involved in** this movie. Ruth, will you **hit play,** and Susan, can you pass the popcorn over here please?

QUESTIONS
1. When you visit friends, do you usually take them something? If yes, what?
2. What do you think a "couch potato" is?
3. What is Michael worried about?
4. What do you think a "tearjerker" can make people do?

■ Understanding the New Expressions

1. gét togéther = join a person or people to socialize

S1: Do you want to **get together** this weekend?
S2: I'd really like to, but let me check my calendar first. I'll call you back.

Note: *Notice the use of get together "with" someone, get together "and" + verb, get together "for" + noun:*

—Let's **get together with** them sometime soon.
—Let's **get together and** have lunch.
—Let's **get together for** lunch.

2. máke oneself cómfortable = an expression that hosts use to welcome their guests

S1: Sit down and **make yourself comfortable.** Can I get you a drink?
S2: Thanks. I'd love one.

Similar expression: to máke oneself at hóme

S1: Come on in and **make yourselves at home.** You can put your coats in there on the bed.
S2: OK. Thanks.

3. **be in the móod to** + **verb** = want to (do something)
be in the mood for + **noun** = want (something)

S1: What do you want to do now?
S2: I'**m in the mood to** eat a hamburger.
   or
   I'**m in the mood for** a hamburger.

Contrast: **be in a góod móod** ≠ **be in a bád móod**

S1: Do you want Chinese or Japanese food tonight?
S2: Whatever you want.
S1: You'**re in a good mood** today. Did something special happen?

S1: Don't go near the boss today.
S2: Why not?
S1: He'**s in a** very **bad mood.**

4. **a téarjerker** = a movie that makes people cry

S1: Do you have a tissue?
S2: I think so. Yeah—here's a clean one. This movie sure is **a tearjerker.**

5. **Hów about** . . . ? = the beginning of a suggestion (in question form)

S1: I don't know what to order.
S2: **How about** the fish? The salads look good, too.

S1: Who should we invite over for dinner?
S2: **How about** Joan and Daniel?

6. **féel líke** *doing something* = **be in the mood to** do something

    S1: What do you **feel like** do**ing?**
    S2: I **feel like** go**ing** to a movie.

       or

    S1: Why didn't you cook tonight?
    S2: I **felt like** order**ing** a pizza instead.

   Contrast:

    S1: How do you feel?
    S2: Fine/Happy/Tired.

7. **be scáred out of one's wíts** = **be scáred to déath** = be extremely frightened
by something
to scáre someone out of his/her wíts = to make someone *very* scared

    S1: How was the movie?
    S2: Don't see it. I **was scared out of my wits.** I had my eyes closed for almost
        the whole time.
    S1: Lots of blood?

    S1: Aaah! Who's that?
    S2: It's only me.
    S1: God! You **scared me out of my wits!** My heart almost stopped.

8. **Thát mákes twó of ús.** = I feel the same way.

    S1: Let's eat. I'm hungry.
    S2: **That makes two of us.**

   Similar expressions:

       With an affirmative statement:

    S1: I like old movies.
    S2: **That makes two of us.**
       or
       So do I.
       or
       Me, too.

       With a negative statement:

    S1: I can't believe it.
    S2: **That makes two of us.**
       or
       Neither can I.
       or
       I can't either.

Are We Couch Potatoes?

9. be (júst) kídding = be joking

S1: I'm going to Hollywood to make horror movies.
S2: Do you have a job?
S1: I **was just kidding.** Did you really believe me?

S1: She won a car.
S2: You**'re kidding!** (or: You **must be kidding!**)
S1: No, I'm not. She really won a car!

Similar expression: You're púlling my lég.

S1: There's going to be an earthquake tomorrow.
S2: **You're pulling my leg.** No one knows when an earthquake will happen.
S1: But I read it in the newspaper.
S2: Don't believe everything you read.

10. móve óver *(inseparable/intransitive)* = move to create space for someone or something

S1: Gail, could you please **move over** a little so someone else can sit down?
S2: Oh, sorry. I didn't realize I was taking up so much space. . . . Here—now you can sit down.

Contrast: móve *something* óver *(to a place)* (must be separated)

S1: If you **move** the couch **over** to the corner, I think the room will look better.
S2: I'd rather **move** it **over** to the window. OK?

11. Hére you gó. = a friendly thing to say when you give someone something

S1: **Here you go.** Can I get you anything else?
S2: Yes. I'd like another cup of coffee.
S1: Sure. I'll be right back.

S1: Mom, can I have some more?
S2: OK, but just a little. **Here you go.**

12. hít páuse/hít pláy = the instruction or request someone might give another person who is either holding a VCR remote control or is near the VCR buttons

S1: Can you **hit pause?** I need to make a quick phone call.
S2: Now? Can't you wait 'til the end of the show?

S1: OK I'm back. You can **hit play.**
S2: I will in a minute, but first I'd like you to tell me why your "quick" call lasted 20 minutes.

13. **a cóuch potato/cóuch potatoes** = people who watch a tremendous amount (lots and lots) of TV

S1: Turn off the TV. You've been watching for six whole hours!
S2: I know. I guess I'm **a couch potato.**

14. **Whý do you ásk?** = Why are you asking me that personal question?

S1: How much money do you have with you?
S2: **Why do you ask?**
S1: I was just curious.

Note: When someone asks you a question that you don't want to answer, you can respond with this question.

15. **spénd (a líttle/a lót of) tíme (do_ing_) something** = use time
(_on_)

S1: He **spends a lot of time** work**ing.** The kids never see him.
S2: Then it's time for a change, isn't it?

S1: You need to **spend more time on** your homework, don't you think?
S2: I guess so.

16. **be glúed to the TV/be glúed to the túbe** = watch TV with such great interest that you can't break away from it, as if you were attached by glue. The **tube** = TV (very informal)

S1: Bobby. Dinner's ready!
S2: He doesn't seem to hear you.
S1: I know. He's always **glued to the tube.** Listen—he won't hear this: Bobby . . . the house is on fire! See—he still didn't hear me.

17. **Thát's fúnny.** = That's strange, unusual.

S1: **That's funny.** I thought I left my keys on the table, but they're nowhere to be seen.
S2: Here they are. They fell.

S1: 20 . . . 25 . . . 26 . . . 27 . . . I only have $27 in my wallet. **That's funny.** Yesterday I had $100 and I don't remember spending that much.
S2: Didn't you go out to dinner last night?
S1: Yeah, but I didn't spend $70!

Contrast: **Thát** _____ **is fúnny.** = Something is humorous—it makes me laugh.

S1: **That** movie **is** really **funny.** You should see it.
S2: I think I will. I need a good laugh.

18. **be a bóokworm** = be someone who reads all the time

S1: Let's go for a walk.
S2: Not now. I'm in the middle of this great book.
S1: You**'re** such **a bookworm.** Every time I look at you, you've got a book in your hands.

19. **pút (a bóok) dówn** (separable/transitive) = stop reading

S1: Dinner's ready.
S2: Start without me. I can't **put this book down.**

S1: Why do you look so tired?
S2: I didn't sleep last night. I was reading a book that I couldn't **put down** until I finished it.

20. **be** (*or* gét) **invólved in** = be (or become) completely interested in what you are reading, watching, or doing

S1: Why don't you turn the TV off?
S2: Because I**'m involved in** this show. I'll turn it off when the show's over.

S1: I thought you were reading that book.
S2: I was, but I put it down. I couldn't **get involved in** it.

Contrast: **be invólved with** *someone* = be in a romantic relationship

S1: **Are** you **involved with** anyone now?
S2: Why do you ask?

1. Mini-Dialogues

Below are two columns, A and B. Column A contains the first lines of dialogues and column B contains possible responses. For each opening line in column A, choose the *best* response from column B.

When checking this exercise in class, perform each mini-dialogue. One student should read an item from column A and another student should respond with the answer from column B.

A

_____ **1.** Come in and make yourselves comfortable.

_____ **2.** I'd like two tickets, please.

_____ **3.** We got married last week.

_____ **4.** Let's get together for coffee.

_____ **5.** I feel like getting some exercise.

_____ **6.** Can you hit pause for a second?

_____ **7.** Were you ever involved with each other?

_____ **8.** She's an hour late.

_____ **9.** You're shaking.

_____ **10.** Your eyes are red.

_____ **11.** Want to dance?

_____ **12.** I need a vacation.

_____ **13.** It's kind of crowded here.

_____ **14.** Put down that book and listen to me!

B

a. Where's the remote?

b. Why do you ask?

c. That car scared me out of my wits.

d. You're kidding!

e. Get your bike and I'll meet you at the park.

f. Sorry. I'm not in the mood right now.

g. Sorry. I was involved.

h. Where should we put our coats?

i. Great idea. How's tomorrow?

j. That's funny. She's always on time. Let's give her a call.

k. Here you go.

l. That makes two of us.

m. I just saw a tearjerker. There wasn't a dry eye in the house.

n. I'll move over.

2. Choosing the Idiom

The following dialogue takes place between the two people in the illustration. Fill in the blanks with some of the expressions on the list. Pay special attention to how the expressions are used grammatically. (You will need to consider verb tenses, subject-verb agreement, plurals, etc.) After you have checked your answers, perform the dialogue with a partner.

you're kidding	spend all my time	in the mood
get together	move over	here you go
feel like	that's funny	a couch potato
that makes two of us	scares me out of my wits	how about

JACK: I'm bored.

JILL: So am I. What do you _____ doing?
(1)

JACK: We could watch TV.

JILL: No. Remember, we promised each other that we'd watch only an hour a day.

You don't want to become _____ , do you?
(2)

JACK: I don't want to _____ reading, either.
(3)

JILL: So, watch a little TV and read a little, too.

JACK: And what will I do with the rest of my time?

JILL: _____ getting some more exercise?
(4)

JACK: I'm never _____ to exercise.
(5)

JILL: _____ , but we should force ourselves to take
(6)

an exercise class.

JACK: _____ !
(7)

JILL: No, I'm not. I'm serious. People our age get heart attacks and it

_____ . We need to get more exercise.
(8)

JACK: _____ . I never thought I'd hear you say that.
(9)

JILL: Well, I saw some shows on TV about the importance of exercise, and . . .

JACK: Oh, so you were watching daytime TV???

JILL: But . . .

3. Dictation

Your teacher or one of your classmates will read the dictation for this unit from Appendix A, or you will listen to the dictation on the audio program. You will hear the dictation three times. First, just listen. Second, as you listen, write the dictation on a separate sheet of paper. Third, as you listen, check what you have written.

4. Any Questions?

Take out a piece of paper. Do NOT write your name on it. On one side of the paper, write down what you think is the most interesting information that you have learned in this lesson up to now. On the other side of the paper, write down any questions that you have about any of the idioms. Your teacher will collect this paper and then answer your questions the next time you meet.

5. Personal Questions

Answer the questions below in a conversation with a partner or in a small group.

1. Do you know any couch potatoes? If yes, who? Are you one? How much TV do you watch every day? Why kind of show is your favorite?

2. Do many people have VCRs and video cameras in your native country? Do people buy and rent video cassettes very often? Do you think people watch more TV now that video is available?

3. Do you think parents should limit how much TV their children watch? Explain.

4. Do you think it is possible for parents to prevent their children from watching TV shows that contain sex and violence? Explain.

5. When you watch a movie that was made in a foreign language, do you prefer subtitles (words in your native language written at the bottom of the screen) or dubbing (words in your native language actually spoken)? Explain.

6. Do you know any bookworms? If yes, who? Are you one? How often do you read a book? What kind of book is your favorite?

6. Skit Writing

In this illustration, the people are attending a meeting of the "Couch Potato Club." The president of the club is making a speech to the group about how wonderful it is to watch at least seven hours of TV a day while eating a lot of "junk food" (potato chips, candy, etc.).

Work individually, in pairs, or as a class to write the president's speech. Try to use at least five new expressions from this lesson and two expressions from previous lessons. Suggested starting line: "*Today, I'm going to talk about why people should be couch potatoes.*"

After you have finished writing the speech, choose someone to give it. The rest of the class can be the couch potato audience. After the speech, they should have a question and answer session with the president.

7. Improvisation

Using the new expressions from this lesson, act out the following role-play. The new expressions should be written on the board.

Imagine that the Couch Potato Club wants to have meetings at your school and wants to get students to join. Do you think that would be a good idea?

Set up a debate. On one side, have students who *want* this club. On the other side, have students who *don't want* this club. Choose one person to be the moderator. This person will *not* express an opinion, but will call on people to speak and make sure that only one person speaks at a time.

Possible starting line for the moderator:
What is one reason why our school should have this club?

(You may want to have one debate in front of the class or many small debates going on at the same time in your classroom. Groups of five are good—two students on each side, with one moderator.)

8. Real Life

Think of situations in your own life in which you might use some of the expressions from this lesson. Write down at least five. Outside of class, remember your list and try to use some of your new vocabulary. Also, when you watch TV and listen to people speak, listen carefully—you may hear these expressions.

Expressions	*Real-Life Situations*
Example: *hit pause/hit play*	*I would say, "Can you please hit play or pause" when watching a videotape and someone else has the remote control.*
1.	
2.	
3.	
4.	
5.	

Forgetting a Date

BOB: Nancy! Uh-oh! Nancy . . . wait!

NANCY: Why should I?

BOB: Listen, I'm really embarrassed about last night. **To be honest with you,** I completely forgot about our date.

NANCY: I know.

BOB: I didn't mean to **hurt your feelings.**

NANCY: But you did. Obviously I wasn't **on your mind.** You **stood me up,** Bob!

BOB: Listen, we can **work this out.** Let me **make up for** it. I'll **treat you to dinner** tonight.

NANCY: Aren't you going to explain what happened?

BOB: I did explain. I forgot to **show up.**

NANCY: Would YOU **stand for** an explanation like that?

BOB: Well, I guess **you've got a point there.** OK. Sit down, and I'll tell you the truth about what happened.

1. Why does Bob say "Uh-oh?" Does he "smell trouble"?
2. How does Nancy feel? Why?
3. Was Bob really honest with her (at first)?
4. Was Nancy satisfied with his explanation? Why?
5. Would YOU be satisfied with Bob's explanation? Why?
6. If you were Bob, what would you have said to Nancy?

■ Understanding the New Expressions

1. **to be hónest with you** = to téll you the trúth

S1: What time should we leave?
S2: **To be honest with you,** I don't want to go.

S1: What's the matter?
S2: **To tell you the truth,** I don't love you any more.

Note: *These expressions often introduce information that is not good news.*

2. **húrt *someone's* féelings** = cause someone to feel bad

S1: I can't believe you didn't call me.
S2: I'm sorry that ⎫ **I hurt your feelings.**
　　　　　　　　 if　⎭

3. **be on *someone's* mínd** = be in someone's thoughts

S1: I'm in love!
S2: How can you be sure?
S1: I can't stop thinking about her. She's **on my mind** twenty-four hours a day!

Contrast: **have *(sómething)* on *(one's)* mínd** = have something serious to think about

S1: Why do you look so serious?
S2: I **have** a lot **on my mind.**

4. **stánd *someone* úp** *(separable/transitive)* = not arrive for a date. Someone who stands up a date does *not* call to cancel.

S1: She said she would meet me at 7:00, and it's already 9:00. I'm so angry!
S2: Maybe something happened to make her late.
S1: No, she didn't even call! She **stood me up!**

Passive form: **be stóod úp**

S1: Why is he so upset?
S2: He **was stood up.**

5. **wórk *something* óut** *(separable/transitive)* = solve a problem

S1: Won't you please talk to me? As the Beatles said, "We can **work it out.**"
S2: Maybe the Beatles can **work out** their problems, but can we?

6. **make úp for** = do something nice as an apology

S1: You're not doing your share of the work. I've cooked dinner every night this week.
S2: I'm really sorry. Tell me how I can **make up for** it.
S1: You can **make up for** it by cooking dinner every night next week!

Contrast: **make úp** *(inseparable/intransitive)* = become friends again

S1: Are Jack and Jill together again?
S2: Yes, they **made up** last week.

> **make úp** *(separable/transitive)* = create

S1: Did she get in trouble for being late?
S2: Nope (No). She **made up** an interesting story ⎫ about why she was late.
                                                                   excuse ⎭

> **mákeup** *(noun)* = cosmetics

S1: Go wash your face! You're wearing too much **makeup** for a girl your age.
S2: But, Dad—everyone wears makeup!

7. **tréat *someone* (to *something*)** = pay for someone's meal in a restaurant or for a ticket to an event.

> **S1:** I'll pay for dinner tonight.
> **S2:** Come on. Let me **treat you** to dinner.
> **S1:** I wanted to **treat YOU!**
> **S2:** You can **treat me** next time.
> *Note:* *When you want to treat someone, you can also say:* ***It's on me*** *or* ***I'll get it.*** *If you want to divide the check equally, you can say:* ***Let's split it*** *(see Lesson 7).*

8. **shów úp** *(inseparable/intransitive)* = arrive, appear

> **S1:** Why is Diane in trouble with Sam?
> **S2:** His party started at 9:00 and she **showed up** at 11:30!

> **S1:** Why are you home so early?
> **S2:** My teacher didn't **show up,** and we didn't have a substitute.

9. **(not) stánd for something** = (not) tolerate some behavior

> **S1:** I'm afraid I'm going to fail this test.
> **S2:** I know you're worried, but don't try to cheat. The teacher **won't stand for** cheating.

Similar expression: **cán't stánd** = hate

> **S1:** I hope it snows. I love the winter.
>
> **S2:** Not me. I **can't stand** { cold weather. / to be cold. / being cold.

> *Note:* *"Stand for" is always followed by a noun or gerund. "Can't stand" is followed by either a noun, an infinitive, or a gerund.*

10. **You've gót a póint (there).** = You said something that I have to agree with.

S1: I think we should take the train to the mountains.

S2: I'd rather drive.

S1: But there's going to be a lot of snow.

S2: I like snow.

S1: Do you like sitting in the car for hours, stuck in the snow?

S2: You've got a point there. Let's take the train.

Note: *In this dialogue, S1 and S2 at first disagreed. Then S1 convinced S2 to change his mind. S2 gave in, or conceded, when he said, "You've got a point there."*

■ Exercises

1. Mini-Dialogues

Below are two columns, A and B. Column A contains the first lines of dialogues and column B contains possible responses. For each opening line in column A, choose the *best* response from column B.

When checking this exercise in class, perform each mini-dialogue. One student should read an item from column A, and another student should respond with the answer from column B.

	A		**B**
_____	**1.** Why are you so upset?	**a.**	Make up an excuse.
_____	**2.** What do you have on your face?	**b.**	They made up.
_____	**3.** Look! They're laughing together. I thought they had a fight.	**c.**	By 6:00.
_____	**4.** How can I make up for what I did?	**d.**	It was his birthday.
_____	**5.** I was absent for no reason. What should I tell the teacher?	**e.**	You hurt my feelings.
_____	**6.** Why did you treat him?	**f.**	All right. What should we do?
_____	**7.** What time should I show up?	**g.**	To be honest with you, I was too tired.
_____	**8.** Why didn't you come to my party?	**h.**	Makeup.
_____	**9.** Talk to me. We can work this out.	**i.**	I have a lot on my mind.
_____	**10.** I'll pick you up at 8:00.	**j.**	Just tell me you're sorry.
_____	**11.** Why do you look so worried?	**k.**	Don't stand me up!
_____	**12.** Why isn't she paying attention?	**l.**	I wouldn't stand for that kind of behavior.
_____	**13.** He's late all the time.	**m.**	She has Bob on her mind.

2. Choosing the Idiom

The following dialogue takes place between the lawyer and the woman in the illustration. Fill in the blanks with some of the expressions on the list. Pay special attention to how the expressions are used grammatically. (You will need to consider verb tenses, subject-verb agreement, plurals, etc.) After you have checked your answers, perform the dialogue with a partner.

can't stand
stand for
stand (someone) up
make up *(use two times)*
make up for
show up

hurt (someone's) feelings
treat (someone)
work it out
to be honest with you
you've got a point there

LAWYER: You must tell the truth here. If you don't, you'll go to prison.

NANCY: I'm not lying to you. I'm not _____ stories. I
                                                                              (1)

did not kill Bob. _____ , I don't know why I'm
                                             (2)

here.

LAWYER: Because you were seen talking to him right before the murder. What were

you talking about?

NANCY: He was embarrassed about forgetting our date and he was trying to

_____ . But I was still angry.
                    (3)

LAWYER: Why?

NANCY: He wasn't telling me the real reason why

he _____ . I told him that I
                    (4)

wouldn't _____ his simple explanation.
                    (5)

I _____ being lied to.
                    (6)

LAWYER: So you killed him.

NANCY: I did not! Finally, he did explain why he

didn't _____ the night before.
                    (7)

LAWYER: Well?

NANCY: You're really embarrassing me. OK. He said that he had met his old

girlfriend unexpectedly and _____ to dinner.
                                        (8)

LAWYER: Aha! So you were jealous and wanted to kill him!

NANCY: Only for a minute. We sat down and talked. He knew he

had _____ and he apologized. We both
                    (9)

wanted to _____ because we loved each
                    (10)

other. Why don't you talk to his ex-girlfriend? She was probably more

jealous than I was!

LAWYER: _____ .
                    (11)

3. Dictation

Your teacher or one of your classmates will read the dictation for this unit from Appendix A, or you will listen to the dictation on the audio program. You will hear the dictation three times. First, just listen. Second, as you listen, write the dictation on a separate sheet of paper. Third, as you listen, check what you have written.

4. Any Questions?

Take out a piece of paper. Do NOT write your name on it. On one side of the paper, write down what you think is the most interesting information that you have learned in this lesson up to now. On the other side of the paper, write down any questions that you have about any of the idioms. Your teacher will collect this paper and then answer your questions the next time you meet.

5. Personal Questions

Answer the questions below in a conversation with a partner or in a small group.

1. Have you ever stood anyone up? If yes, what happened?

2. Has anyone ever stood you up? if yes, what happened?

3. When you have a lot on your mind, are you hard to live with? Why or why not?

4. Describe what happened when someone hurt your feelings.

5. What are two things that you can't stand?

6. What do you think a teacher should do if a student shows up late in class? In your native country, what happens if a student

> shows up late?
> eats in class?
> reads the newspaper in class?
> talks to another student?
> cheats on a test?

6. Skit Writing

In this illustration, Nancy (from the two dialogues in this lesson) tells her best friends, Don and Janet, about her argument with Bob and her subsequent arrest for his murder. Nancy describes the trial and how happy she was when the jury announced that she was innocent. Don explains that he and Janet were told nothing about Nancy's problems when they were away on a trip, and asks Nancy for all of the details of her experience.

Work individually, in pairs, or as a class to write their conversation. Try to use at least five new expressions from this lesson and two expressions from previous lessons. After you have finished, perform the "skit" you created for your class.

7. Improvisation

Using the new expressions from this lesson, act out the following role-play. The new expressions should be written on the board.

You and a friend are standing in front of a theater, waiting for two other friends. These friends have the tickets to the concert that you plan to attend. You wait and wait, and start to get upset.

Possible starting lines:
They should be here by now. Where are they?

or

I hope we find them in this crowd.

8. Real Life

Think of situations in your own life in which you might use some of the expressions from this lesson. Write down at least five. Outside of class, remember your list and try to use some of your new vocabulary. Also, when you watch TV and listen to people speak, listen carefully—you may hear these expressions.

Expressions	*Real-Life Situations*
Example: *to be honest with you*	*when I have to tell close friends something that they don't want to hear—that they hurt my feelings, or that they are wearing something that I don't like*
1.	
2.	
3.	
4.	
5.	

For Here or to Go?

MOLLIE:	The line sure is long.
RONNIE:	Well, we're not in a hurry. What are you going to . . . Did you see that? That guy **cut in line.**
MOLLIE:	I can't believe people like that. It's a good thing we're not in a hurry. Anyway, lunch **is on me** today.
RONNIE:	Uh-uh. **It's my turn.**
MOLLIE:	No, it isn't! You treat me every time we **eat out.**
RONNIE:	Why don't we compromise and **split it** then?
MOLLIE:	Because I'm treating you, and **that's that.**

❖ ❖ ❖ ❖ ❖

MOLLIE:	One hamburger, one chicken sandwich, two small fries, and two cokes.
COUNTERPERSON:	Is that **for here or to go?**
MOLLIE:	For here.

❖ ❖ ❖ ❖ ❖

MOLLIE: Do you know what Casey **is up to** these days?

RONNIE: **You got me.**

MOLLIE: He's **taking a** quit-smoking **class.**

RONNIE: **It's about time.** He's the only one I know who still smokes.

MOLLIE: Ronnie, **don't be so hard on** him. You know he's tried almost everything—gum, hypnosis. He's even **gone cold turkey.**

RONNIE: I hope he . . . **Look who's here** . . . Hey, Casey! Over here!

MOLLIE: **Speak of the devil!**

CASEY: Were you talking about me?

MOLLIE: Yeah, I was telling Ronnie about the class you're taking.

CASEY: Well, that's no secret. I **figure** if I tell everyone I know that I'm taking that class, they won't let me smoke.

RONNIE: Not a bad idea. **How's it going?**

CASEY: Pretty well **so far. I've got a long way to go.** But I've **made a promise to** myself—I'm not going to **give up** this time—I'm not going to **end up** be**ing** the only smoker in this town.

QUESTIONS
1. Do you ever eat fast food? Why or why not?
2. What do you do or say if someone **cuts in line** in front of you?
3. What do you think **for here or to go** means?
4. Do you think Mollie, Ronnie, and Casey are good friends? Why or why not?

■ Understanding the New Expressions

1. cút in líne = join a line of people somewhere in the middle, not at the end

S1: Let's **cut in line** to make sure that we get into the theater.
S2: No way. How can you even think of doing that? I'm going to the back of the line.

Contrast: **gét in líne** = join the end of a line of people

S1: Why don't you **get in line** while I park the car?
S2: Good idea.

Note: *In some areas of the U.S., it is common to say get "on" line.*

2. **(It's) on mé** = I will pay

S1: Dinner **is on me** tonight.
S2: No, you shouldn't . . .
S1: No argument. It's my pleasure.
S2: Thank you.

Note: When someone offers to pay for you, it's common first to resist (disagree), but then to accept and thank him or her.

3. **Lét's splít it.** = You pay half, and I'll pay half. ("it" = the check)

S1: Let me treat you. (*Or:* It's on me.)
S2: No, **let's split it.** This restaurant is so expensive.
S1: All right, but let me pay the tip.

Note: You can also say: **Lét's splít the chéck.**
or
Lét's splít the táb. ("tab" is very informal)
or
Lét's gó Dútch. (This expression is not very common today.)

Contrast: **Lét's splít.** = Let's leave. *This has* **nothing** *to do with paying; it's a very informal expression that young people often use to say, "Let's leave."*

4. **It's mý turn (to)** = This time *I* will do something because you did it last time.

S1: **It's my turn to** drive, so I'll pick you up.
S2: I'll be waiting for you on the corner.

Similar expression: to táke túrns _____ing

S1: It's a long trip, so we should **take turns** driv**ing,** don't you think?
S2: Absolutely.

5. **éat óut** (inseparable/intransitive) = eat in a restaurant

S1: Let's **eat out tonight. I don't feel like cooking.**
S2: Great idea. How about Chinese food?

Similar Expression: go óut to éat

—Let's **go out to eat** tonight. I don't feel like cooking.

6. Thát's thát. = **Thát's fínal.** = That is the end of the discussion. The decision has been made.

> **S1 (child):** I want to go to the movies.
> **S2 (child):** I want to go to the beach.
> **S3 (child):** I want to go to the park.
> **S4 (parent):** We're going to go home, and **that's that.**

> *Note:* To be polite with another adult, say this only if you are insisting on doing something nice, such as treating in a restaurant.

7. For hére or to gó? = Do you want to eat in the restaurant, or do you want to take your food out in a bag so you can eat it somewhere else?

> **S1: For here or to go?**
> **S2: To go,** please.

> *Similar Expression:* **Is this to go?**

8. be úp to = be busy with, be doing

> **S1:** What **are** you **up to?**
> **S2:** Nothing much. Just the regular routine.

> **S1:** What **are** you **up to?**
> **S2:** Spring cleaning. It's a big job.

> *Contrast:* **nót be up to** _____**ing** = not have the energy to do something

> **S1:** Let's go.
> **S2:** I'm going to stay home. **I'm not up to goíng** out. I'm too tired.

> *Contrast:* **Whát's úp?** = What's happening? What's new?
> *or*
> What's the matter?

> **S1:** Hi, Casey! **What's up?**
> **S2:** Nothing much. I'm still taking that class.

> **S1:** Mollie, you look really upset. **What's up?** (What's the matter?)
> **S2:** I'm worried about my test—it was really hard.

9. You gót mé. (Or: You've got me.) = I have *no* idea. I don't know.

> **S1:** Where's the dog?
> **S2: You got me.**

> *Note:* This is an **informal** way to answer a question asked by someone you know very well.

10. táke a cláss/táke clásses

> **S1:** What are you **taking** this semester?
> **S2:** English, math, history, and biology.
>
> **S1:** I'm **taking** two P.E. (physical education) **classes** this semester, and they're a lot of fun.
> **S2:** What are you **taking?**
> **S1:** Tennis and swimming.

Similar Expression: táke a tést/táke tésts (See Lesson 9.)

—Whenever I **take a test,** I get really nervous.
—When you **take tests,** be sure to keep your eyes on your own paper.

11. It's abóut tíme (that) = Something has just happened or someone has just done something that should have happened or been done before.

> **S1:** The bus is finally here, and **it's about time.** Twenty minutes late!
> **S2:** Next time, let's drive instead.
>
> **S1:** **It's about time that** she stopped smoking. She should have stopped a long time ago.
> **S2:** She tried, but she couldn't.

Note: *This expression is said with some anger because someone or something is late.*

12. Dón't be só hárd on *someone* = Don't be so mean or strict

> **S1:(father)** You're late again. It's 2:00 a.m. and you were supposed to be home by midnight.
> **S2:(son or daughter)** Sorry, Dad. I didn't have my watch.
> **S1:(father)** That's no excuse. You're not going out again at night for a month.
> **S3:(mother)** **Don't be so hard on him/her!** A month is a long time.

13. qúit *or* gó cóld túrkey = suddenly and completely stop doing something addictive such as taking drugs, drinking alcohol, or smoking

S1: Maybe you should try to smoke a little less every day.

S2: That won't work. I have to **quit cold turkey.** I'm going to throw this pack of cigarettes into the garbage right now and never smoke another cigarette again in my life.

S1: Are you going to go to a quit smoking class?

S2: No, I'm going to **go cold turkey** without any help.

14. **Lóok who's hére!** = Look at who just arrived.

—**Look who's here!** I can't believe it! It's great to see you.

15. **Spéak of the dévil!** = This expression is used when the person you are talking about arrives or you see the person while you are in the middle of talking about him or her.

S1: Jennifer is going to be famous some day. She really is a great actress.

S2: I know. And she can sing, too. Have you ever heard her?

S1: Oh, yes. About a year ago . . . **Speak of the devil!** There she is. Should we invite her to join us?

16. **to fígure** = to think (informal)

S1: I **figure,** if I save $50 a month, I still won't have enough to travel.

S2: Try to save $100. You can do it.

17. **Hów's it góing?** = How is something that you already started progressing? (informal)

S1: I just started swimming every day.

S2: **How's it going?**

S1: Pretty well.

S1: I'm finally taking a computer class.

S2: **How's it going?**

S1: Hi! **How's it going?**
S2: Not bad. How are you?

18. **só fár** = until now, up to a point

S1: How do you like the book?
S2: I've only read a few pages. **So far** I think I like it, but I'm not really sure.

Similar expression: **só fár, só góod** = until now, something is good or going well

S1: How's the book?
S2: **So far, so good.**

19. **have (got) a lóng wáy to gó** = be far away from your goal

S1: You've made a lot of progress so far.
S2: Thanks a lot, but I **have a long way to go.**

20. **máke a prómise/máke prómises (to *someone*)** = promise

S1: She always **makes promises** that she doesn't keep.
S2: I know what you mean. It's hard to trust what she says.

Similar expressions: **to kéep a prómise** ≠ **to bréak a prómise**

S1: I promise that I will do my homework every night, and that I will do it well.
S2: I hope that you will **keep your promise.**
S1: I never **break a promise.** Believe me.

21. **gíve úp** (inseparable/intransitive) = stop trying to do something

S1: I **give up!** I can't do it. I've been practicing pronunciation every day and people still don't understand me.
S2: Don't **give up** so fast. You need to be more patient.

Contrast: **gíve úp (something)** (separable/transitive) = quit, break a bad habit

S1: They are going to **give up** smok**ing** so their children won't imitate them.
S2: That's good to hear.

22. **énd úp** (+ _____ **ing**) = finally become, have, or do something

—She's really interested in biology. I bet she'll **end up** becom**ing** a doctor.
—At the party we started out being nervous, but we **ended up** hav**ing** fun.
—We were going to go to the movies, but we **ended up** go**ing** out to eat.

Note: *"End up" usually shows that a change occurs. Notice the following about the three sentences above:*

be interested in biology → end up becoming a doctor
be nervous → end up having fun
plan to go to the movies → end up going out to eat

Some more examples:
—They started out happy but **ended up** gett**ing** a divorce.
—At first he loved his job, but he **ended up** hat**ing** it.
—At first she hated her job, but she **ended up** lov**ing** it.

■ Exercises

1. Mini-Dialogues

Below are two columns, A and B. Column A contains the first lines of dialogues and column B contains possible responses. For each opening line in column A, choose the *best* response from column B.

When checking this exercise in class, perform each mini-dialogue. One student should read an item from column A and another student should respond with the answer from column B.

A	B
_____ **1.** It's on me.	**a.** Don't be so hard on me.
_____ **2.** For here or to go?	**b.** Yeah. I heard they ended up getting married.
_____ **3.** Let's cut in line.	**c.** So far, so good.
_____ **4.** You never do anything right.	**d.** Speak of the devil! There he is right now!
_____ **5.** Look who's here!	**e.** It's about time. We've been sitting here for 20 minutes.
_____ **6.** Remember Andrea and Gregory?	**f.** I know. We'd better see what she's up to.
_____ **7.** How's it going?	**g.** Amy and Kirk—It's great to see you!
_____ **8.** Doctor, will he be OK?	**h.** You got me!
_____ **9.** Have you seen Bill? He cut his hair.	**i.** Yes. He's made a lot of progress. But he's still got a long way to go.
_____ **10.** Let me ride the bike a little longer.	**j.** No—let's split it.
_____ **11.** Here comes the waitress.	**k.** No way. I hate when people do that to me.
_____ **12.** What's Aaron doing today?	**l.** Yeah, it's getting expensive.
_____ **13.** Come on. Just one more time.	**m.** He's taking a computer class.
_____ **14.** Let's split. I'm tired.	**n.** I said no, and that's that!
_____ **15.** I think we eat out too much.	**o.** No! It's my turn.
_____ **16.** The baby's too quiet.	**p.** Don't give up. Try again.
_____ **17.** I can't do it.	**q.** Me, too.
_____ **18.** How does this thing work?	**r.** To go, please.

2. Choosing the Idiom

The following conversation takes place between the people in the illustration. Fill in the blanks with some of the expressions on the list. Pay special attention to how the expressions are used grammatically. (You will need to consider verb tenses, subject-verb agreement, plurals, etc.) After you have checked your answers, perform the dialogue with a partner.

figure	so far, so good	take this class
end up	it's on me	look who's here
eat out	you got me	make a promise
it's my turn	let's split it	how's it going

CHERYL: I'm so glad I'm _____ .
                                        (1)

I _____ to myself to come here at least five
                (2)

times a week.

KATE: That often? You'll _____ with big muscles!
                                        (3)

CHERYL: I just want to be healthy. I _____ if I come
                                                    (4)

here a lot, the exercises will become easier for me.

Hey— _____ —Virginia—are you taking a
                    (5)

class here?

VIRGINIA: Hi, _____ ?
                            (6)

CHERYL: Fine. Are you taking a class here?

VIRGINIA: I'm not really sure. I was just taking a look. How is the class?

CHERYL: _____(7)_____ . We've had only two classes, and

my muscles really hurt.

KATE: Mine do, too, but it feels good. Listen, why don't we go out for lunch. Are

you free?

CHERYL: I'm free, but I can't _____(8)_____ because I'm trying

to save money.

KATE: No problem. _____(9)_____ .

CHERYL: Thanks, Kate, but I really have a lot to do anyway this afternoon. Maybe

some other time.

KATE: How about you, Virginia?

VIRGINIA: I'll be free around one. Do you want to meet at the deli?

3. Dictation

Your teacher or one of your classmates will read the dictation for this unit from Appendix A, or you will listen to the dictation on the audio program. You will hear the dictation three times. First, just listen. Second, as you listen, write the dictation on a separate sheet of paper. Third, as you listen, check what you have written.

4. Any Questions?

Take out a piece of paper. Do NOT write your name on it. On one side of the paper, write down what you think is the most interesting information that you have learned in this lesson up to now. On the other side of the paper, write down any questions that you have about any of the idioms. Your teacher will collect this paper and then answer your questions the next time you meet.

5. Personal Questions

Answer the questions below in a conversation with a partner or in a small group.

1. Are you the kind of person who will cut in line? If yes, describe a situation in which you did this.

2. If someone cuts in line in front of you, do you say anything? If yes, what?

3. If you go out to eat or to have a drink with your friends in your native country, does one person usually treat the others or do you usually split the check? Do women ever treat men? What is the "system"?

4. In the U.S., it is common to do the following:

(a) go to a fast-food restaurant and order food "to go."

(b) call a Chinese restaurant on the phone and order a meal. Then, about fifteen minutes later, you pick up your meal and eat it at home.

(c) call a pizza place and order a pizza to be delivered. About a half hour later, someone brings a pizza to your house.

(d) eat at a restaurant and then ask for a "doggie bag" or a container for the food you haven't finished. You take this extra food home and eat it at another time. This is done so that the food is not wasted. (In the past, people took meat bones home to their dogs in "doggie bags," but people now do not hide the fact that they want to take home "leftover" food for themselves.)

Are any of the above customs surprising to you? If yes, which ones and why? Do you have any of the same customs in your native country? If yes, which ones?

5. In English, people often say, "Speak of the devil" when the person that they are talking about suddenly appears. In your native language, is there an expression similar to this one? If yes, what does the expression mean in English?

6. Do people in your native country take "self-improvement" classes such as classes that help people quit smoking? Are exercise classes common? Why or why not?

7. Tell your group about a promise that you once made and kept.
Tell your group about a promise that you once made but broke.

6. Skit Writing

In this illustration, Casey's doctor is listening to his lungs. The doctor is very pleased because Casey has quit smoking and is also getting a lot of exercise. The doctor asks Casey questions about his daily life.

Work individually, in pairs, or as a class to write their conversation. Try to use at least five new expressions from this lesson and two expressions from previous lessons. After you have finished, perform the "skit" you created for your class.

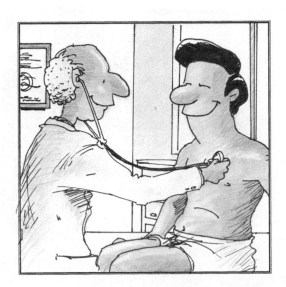

For Here or to Go?

7. Improvisation

Using the new expressions from this lesson, act out the following role-play. The new expressions should be written on the board.

You and a few friends are eating at a restaurant. You are talking about a friend who is not there—you decide what you are saying about this person.

Suddenly, this person walks in. He or she joins you.

After you finish eating, the waiter brings the check and two or three of you want to pay. You argue at first, but then decide if one person will pay or if you will split the check.

Possible starting line:
Have you heard about _____ ? S/he is . . .

8. Real Life

Think of situations in your own life in which you might use some of the expressions from this lesson. Write down at least five. Outside of class, remember your list and try to use some of your new vocabulary. Also, when you watch TV and listen to people speak, listen carefully—you may hear these expressions.

Expressions	*Real-Life Situations*
Example: *For here or to go?*	*I would be asked this in fast-food restaurants and also in cafés where tea and coffee are sold.*

1.

2.

3.

4.

5.

How About Going to a Movie?

ROSEMARY:	Hello?
FRANK:	Hi, Rosemary. This is Frank. How're you doing?
ROSEMARY:	OK, but busy.
FRANK:	Can you **make time to** go to a movie this afternoon?
ROSEMARY:	I wish I could, but I have a lot of homework. I'll have to **take a rain check.**
FRANK:	Come on, **take** some **time off.** You're always studying! You're going to **turn into** a robot **before you know it.**
ROSEMARY:	Well, I have a lot to do. Don't you have work to do?
FRANK:	I did, but I **got** it **over with,** so I can leave early. . . . Listen, it's my birthday.
ROSEMARY:	Really? I didn't know! Happy birthday!

FRANK: Thanks. I wanted to celebrate it with you.

ROSEMARY: Well, **when you put it that way,** how can I refuse? You **talked me into** it.

FRANK: Great. You don't know how glad I am that you **changed your mind.**

QUESTIONS
1. Why is Frank able to leave work early?
2. Do you think that Rosemary is really busy?
3. What kind of relationship do you think Rosemary and Frank really have? How long do you think they have known each other?
4. Why did Rosemary change her mind?

■ Understanding the New Expressions

1. máke (some) tíme to do *something* = provide time in a schedule to do something specific

S1: I have to clean my house, do my laundry, make dinner, do my homework . . .
S2: How are you going to **make time to** sleep?

máke (some) tíme for *someone or something*

S1: I'm sorry. The dentist is very busy today. Can you come in tomorrow?
S2: Can't he **make some time for** me? I have a terrible toothache.

2. táke a ráin check = ask if you can accept an invitation at a future time

S1: Can you come over for dinner tonight?
S2: I'm sorry, I can't. Can I **take a rain check?**

S1: Didn't they invite him to go swimming?
S2: Uh-huh. But he has a cold, so he had to **take a rain check.**

gíve (*somebody*) a ráin check

S1: Can you come over for dinner tonight?
S2: I'm sorry, I can't. Can you **give me a rain check** for next week?

Note: *This expression has a literal origin. When you plan to attend an outdoor sports event and it rains, you are given a "rain check" so that you can attend a future event without paying again.*

3. táke (*tíme*) off (*usually separated/transitive*) = stop work for a day or more for rest or any other personal reason

S1: I need a vacation.
S2: Why don't you **take** some time **off?**
S1: I'll think about it.

Similar expressions: táke a bréak/cóffee break

S1: I've been sitting at this desk for two hours. I need to **take a break.**
S2: Me, too. Come on. It's time for our **coffee break.**

Note: *"To take a break" is to stop work for a short time, usually from a few minutes to an hour; "to take time off" is to stop work for a longer period of time, usually a day or more.*

4. túrn ínto *something* (*inseparable/transitive*) = become something different

S1: What happened?
S2: The milk in my refrigerator **turned into** ice.

túrn *something* ínto *something* (*separable/transitive*)

S1: The cold weather **turned** the lake **into** an ice skating rink.
S2: I hope warm weather will **turn** it **into** water again soon.

5. **befóre (you) knów it** = very soon—before a person realizes something

S1: Time is really flying.
S2: It sure is. School will be over (finished) **before we know it.**

S1: Why are they so wet?
S2: It started to rain, and **before they knew it,** they were walking in a foot of water.

Note: *When this expression is at the beginning or middle of a sentence, it is always followed by a comma: Before you know it, school will be over.*

6. **gét** *something* **óver with** *(must be separated)* = Do something you don't enjoy so you won't have to do it later

S1: Some people say, "Don't do tomorrow what you can do today." I say, "Don't do today what you can do tomorrow."
S2: I'm different. When I have something to do, like cleaning or work, I like to **get it over with.** Then I can relax.

Note: *Here are some examples of things you might want to "get over with": shopping, cooking, homework, a difficult conversation, a visit or phone call that you don't want to make.*

7. **whén you pút it thát wáy** = This is said when you are given an explanation that convinces you.

S1: Your grades should be higher, Joe. I'm very disappointed in you.
S2: Sorry, Dad. But I have three hours hours of soccer practice every day, and no time to study.
S1: Make time to study. If your grades don't improve, you'll have to stop playing soccer.
S2: **When you put it that way,** I guess I have no choice.

8. **tálk** *someone* **ínto** *doing something* ≠ **tálk** *someone* **óut of** *doing something* = convince someone to do or not do something

S1: What are you doing here? I thought you were going to stay home.
S2: Lisa **talked** me **into** coming.

S1: I thought you were going away this weekend.
S2: I was going to go mountain climbing, but my brother **talked** me **out of** it because the weather is so bad.

Note: *These expressions are followed by gerunds (verb + ing) or the pronoun "it."*

9. **chánge** *one's* **mínd(s)** = decide to do something else

S1: What happened? We waited for you at the café.
S2: I'm sorry. I was planning to join you, but I **changed** my **mind.** I went to the library instead.

S1: Aren't you expecting friends?
S2: They were supposed to arrive today, but they **changed** their **minds.** They're going to come tomorrow.

■ *Exercises*

1. Mini-Dialogues

Below are two columns, A and B. Column A contains the first lines of dialogues and column B contains possible responses. For each opening line in column A, choose the *best* response from column B.

When checking this exercise in class, perform each mini-dialogue. One student should read an item from column A and another student should respond with the answer from column B.

A	B
_____ 1. I have to work late tonight.	a. I got my exams over with and I think I did pretty well.
_____ 2. How'd you like to go to a concert tonight?	b. Maybe. But before you know it, it will be over.
_____ 3. You can have the bike for half price.	c. Again? But you promised to make time to be with the kids.
_____ 4. What're you doing here? I thought you couldn't come.	d. Yes. He's really turned into a nice young man, hasn't he?
_____ 5. You look great! Where have you been?	e. You talked me into it. I'll take it.
_____ 6. A month is a long time for a vacation.	f. They're crazy. We'd better talk them out of it.
_____ 7. Have you seen Bobby lately?	g. I changed my mind when she told me it was free.
_____ 8. They're planning to go swimming where there are sharks.	h. A lot of places. I took a month off to relax.
_____ 9. Why do you look so happy?	i. I'd really like to, but can you give me a rain check? I don't feel very well.

2. Choosing the Idiom

The following dialogue takes place between Cinderella and her fairy godmother in the illustration. Fill in the blanks with some of the expressions on the list. Pay special attention to how the expressions are used grammatically. (You will need to consider verb tenses, subject-verb agreement, plurals, etc.) After you have checked your answers, perform the dialogue with a partner.

make some time for
take some time off
talk (someone) into
turn (someone) into
change (someone's) mind

take a rain check
give (someone) a rain check
get (something) over with
before you know it
when you put it that way

GODMOTHER: Cinderella, come here. I want

to _____ a beautiful princess so that you
           (1)

can go to the prince's ball.

CINDERELLA: Thanks, Fairy Godmother, but can

I _____ ? I have to
        (2)

_____ this cleaning
        (3a)

_____ before my
              (3b)

stepmother and stepsisters come home.

GODMOTHER: No, Cinderella! I won't _____ .
                                              (4)

_____ fun! _____
              (5)   (6)

you'll be an old woman. Enjoy life while you're young. You're

always working. _____ !
                                  (7)

CINDERELLA: _____ , how can I refuse? OK, change
                                    (8)

me.

GODMOTHER: It took you a long time to _____ . OK.
                                        (9)

Stand straight and I'll wave my magic wand. ABRACADABRA!

CINDERELLA: Oh, Fairy Godmother! I'm so glad

you _____ going to the ball! Let's get
                       (10)

going!

3. Dictation

Your teacher or one of your classmates will read the dictation for this unit from Appendix A, or you will listen to the dictation on the audio program. You will hear the dictation three times. First, just listen. Second, as you listen, write the dictation on a separate sheet of paper. Third, as you listen, check what you have written.

4. Any Questions?

Take out a piece of paper. Do NOT write your name on it. On one side of the paper, write down what you think is the most interesting information that you have learned in this lesson up to now. On the other side of the paper, write down any questions that you have about any of the idioms. Your teacher will collect this paper and then answer your questions the next time you meet.

5. Personal Questions

Answer the questions below in a conversation with a partner or in a small group.

1. Are you the kind of person who gets things such as laundry and homework over with, or do you say you'll do those things tomorrow? Which way is it better to be and why?

2. Imagine that you really want to go away for the weekend with your friend. But your friend doesn't want to go. Are you the kind of person who would try to talk your friend into going, or would you just forget the idea the first time your friend says no? If you would try to talk your friend into going, what would you say?

3. Have you ever tried to talk someone out of getting married, getting divorced, quitting a job, taking a job, quitting school, gambling, going somewhere, etc.? What happened?

4. Think about the friends that you had when you were a child. What are two of them like today? In other words, what have they turned into?

5. Do you think that, in general, parents make enough time for their children? Why or why not?

6. Skit Writing

In this illustration, Ms. Hardworker, the president of a large international corporation, is working at her desk. She has been working for ten hours without stopping. She never takes time off to rest, and she looks very tired. Her secretary, Bill, tries to talk her into going home.

Work individually, in pairs, or as a class to write their conversation. Try to use at least five new expressions from this lesson and two expressions from previous lessons. After you have finished, perform the "skit" you created for your class.

7. Improvisation

Using the new expressions from this lesson, act out the following role-play. The expressions should be written on the board.

You and your roommate are studying. Two of your friends come into your room and tell you about a great, scary movie that you shouldn't miss. They try to convince you to go to the movie, mainly because you are the only one of the four who has a car. But you need to finish a report which is due Monday, and your roommate has an exam tomorrow.

Possible starting lines after someone knocks on the door:
Who is it?

or

Come on in, whoever you are.

8. Real Life

Think of situations in your own life in which you might use some of the expressions from this lesson. Write down at least five. Outside of class, remember your list and try to use some of your new vocabulary. Also, when you watch TV and listen to people speak, listen carefully—you may hear these expressions.

Expressions	*Real-Life Situations*
Example: *take some time off*	*when I see a friend or relative who looks very tired from working too hard.*

1.

2.

3.

4.

5.

Crossword Puzzle

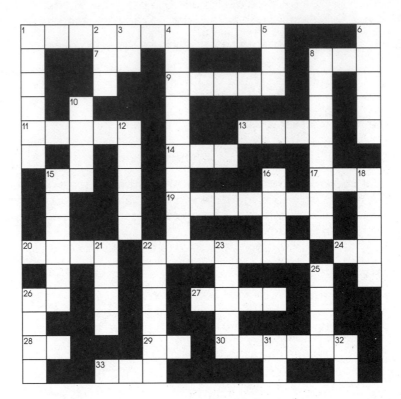

Across

1. Come on in. Make yourselves _____ .

7. It's _____ me.

8. So _____ , the weather has been pretty good.

9. How _____ going to the zoo?

11. She's been _____ to the TV for three hours.

13. I _____ like going out for a while, don't you?

14. Your explanation is so clear—maybe you'll _____ up being a teacher.

15. To _____ honest with you, I didn't really like the movie.

17. I will _____ change my mind.

19. She's _____ —she said she was able to run 50 miles in twenty minutes.

20. He isn't in a _____ mood, so don't talk to him now.

22. They made a _____ to the children that they would take them to the beach.

24. I have a lot _____ my mind.

26. Put your wallet away. It's on _____ .

27. Let's get this work _____ with so we can go out and have a good time.

28. Speak _____ the devil! We were just talking about you.

29. I'm sorry, but I'm not up _____ going. I'm too tired.

30. That noise _____ me out of my wits.

33. That makes _____ of us. I was scared, too.

Down

1. I hope you won't _____ your mind again.

2. Will that be _____ here or to go?

3. same as 7 across

4. What a _____ . I couldn't stop crying!

5. Let's _____ out every Friday night.

6. Come on. Let me _____ you to a cup of coffee.

8. If I hurt your _____ , I'm sorry.

10. Turn off the _____ and read a book.

12. Speak of the _____ —it's you!

15. Enjoy yourself now. _____ you know it, you'll be a lot older.

16. The earthquake scared everyone out of their _____ .

18. Let's take _____ driving because it's a long trip.

21. _____ be so hard on yourself. Take a break.

22. Look—the couch _____ is asleep in front of the TV.

23. When he _____ over in bed, his wife falls on the floor.

25. Would you like that to be for _____ or to go?

26. What are you in the _____ for?

31. Make yourself _____ home.

32. Why _____ you ask? Are you married?

Tic Tac Toe

In this variation of tic tac toe, to get an X or an O you must create a grammatically correct sentence that is logical in meaning. Here is a game to start you off. Create as many games as you like, using expressions from Lessons 5–8.

cut in line	talk somebody out of	get something over with
That's funny	eat out	have a long way to go
show up	give a rain check	put ___ book down

Guess the Idiom

Look at these cartoons and try to guess which expressions from Lessons 5–8 they represent.

1. _____

2. _____

3. _____

4. _____

Review Games for Lessons 5–8

5. _____

6. _____

Pulling an All-Nighter

ALAN:	Why do you look so tired?

ALAN: Why do you look so tired?

ANNETTE: I **pulled an all-nighter** writing my report.

ALAN: Did you finish it?

ANNETTE: Yeah, just **in the nick of time.** I finished typing it a half hour ago, and I have to **turn it in** in five minutes. I'd better hurry.

ALAN: OK. See you later.

(A FEW HOURS LATER)

ANNETTE: Alan—I'm really **in hot water.** My teacher gave us a **pop quiz** and I couldn't remember anything. **My mind went** totally **blank.**

ALAN: Because you didn't **get any sleep.**

ANNETTE: That's right. And he read my report while I was **taking the quiz.** When the quiz **was over,** he asked to see me. He told me to **type** my report **over again** because it's such a mess. He wants me to **hand it in** tomorrow.

ALAN:	I think you'd better **take a nap** before you do any more work today.
ANNETTE:	That's good advice, but I have another class at 2:00, and we're going to have a test.
ALAN:	Another test? You sure **are under** a lot of **pressure.**
ANNETTE:	**You can say that again.** I think I'd better go **hit the books** at the library because I don't want to **take the test cold.**
ALAN:	You mean you didn't study for the test?
ANNETTE:	How could I? I was writing my report!

QUESTIONS
1. Did Annette get any sleep last night? How do you know?
2. In your native country, do students ever stay up all night studying? If yes, when does this happen and how do they stay awake?
3. What is Alan surprised about?

■ Understanding the New Expressions

1. to púll an all-nígher = to stay awake all night to study

S1: I can't believe that the test is in only two weeks.
S2: Neither can I. I'm going to study a little bit every night so I won't have **to pull an all-nighter** the night before the test.
S1: So am I. I never do well if I don't sleep the night before.

Contrast: **stáy úp** = not go to bed (for any reason) (See Lesson 10.)

Similar expression: **to búrn the mídnight óil** = stay up very late working or studying

Note: *This is an old-fashioned expression that is not very common, but you may hear it. It comes from the time when people used oil lamps for light. It does not mean that someone will stay awake all night; it means that someone will go to bed very late after working or studying.*

Similar verb: **to crám** (for a test) = to push a lot of information into your mind at one time; to study "at the last minute"

S1: I'm sorry. I can't talk to you right now. I have to go **cram** for the history midterm. Have you started studying for it yet?
S2: Uh-huh. I forced myself to start over the weekend.
S1: I wish I had done that. I have to read 150 pages and memorize all those dates. I'd better get started.

2. **in the níck of tíme** = just in time; at the last possible moment

—We got here **in the nick of time.** The movie just started.
—You got here **in the nick of time.** We almost left without you.
—They got out of the house **in the nick of time.** The fire reached their house as soon as they were on the street.

Note: *When people do something in the nick of time, they feel relieved.*

3. **túrn ín** *something*/**hánd ín** *something* (*separable/transitive*) = submit; give work to a teacher

S1: I'm so busy, I don't know what to do first.
S2: What do you have to do?
S1: I have to **turn in** two papers by next Tuesday.
S2: I know how you feel. I just **handed** two **in** last week.

Contrast:

> **hánd óut** (*separable/transitive*) = give out; a teacher or helper hands out papers to a class

S1: Please clear your desks. I'm ready to **hand** the quizzes **out.**
S2: How much time will we have for the quiz?

> **hándout** (*noun,* used in school situations) = lesson material on a sheet of paper that a teacher gives to each student

S1: What book are you using in your English class?
S2: No book. The teacher gives us lots of **handouts** instead.

> **hánd báck** (*separable, transitive*) = return, give back student papers that had been turned in

S1: When will you **hand back** our tests?
S2: I'll **hand** them **back** in a few days.

4. **be in hót wáter (with** *someone***)** = be in trouble

S1: What's wrong with her today? She looks so unhappy.
S2: She's **in hot water with** her teacher because she cheated on her test.

5. **a póp qúiz** = a surprise, unexpected quiz

S1: Do you give **pop quizzes** in this class?
S2: Yes, once in a while. I do that so you will study regularly, not just before tests.

Note: *A quiz is a small test. A test is also called an* **exam,** *or more formally, an* **examination.**

6. my mínd wént (tótally) blánk = I couldn't remember anything

—At first, when I looked at the test, **my mind went blank.** So, to calm down, I closed my eyes for a minute or two. Then everything (the information that I had studied) **came back to me.**

Note: *a "blank" is an empty space. If your mind "goes blank," your mind suddenly (and temporarily) feels empty.*

7. gét _____ sléep = sleep

S1: Go to bed! If you don't **get any sleep,** you won't be able to get up in the morning.
S2: I can't go to bed now. I have to read at least three more chapters.

Note: *This expression is usually used the following ways:*

> get some sleep
> get enough sleep
> get a litte/lot of sleep
> *not* get any sleep
> *not* get enough sleep

8. táke a quíz/test

—Please don't make any noise. The students are **taking a test.**

Note the sequence:

> A teacher **makes up** (creates) a test.
> The teacher then **gives** the test to the class.
> Students **take** the test.
> The teacher **corrects** the test and then **hands** it **back.**
> The teacher **goes over** (reviews) the test with the students after they receive their graded tests back.

Note: *It is incorrect to say: The students $\left\{ \begin{array}{c} do \\ make \end{array} \right\}$ a test.*

9. be óver = be finished

S1: I'll do my homework when this show **is over.**
S2: No, you'll do your homework now! Turn off the TV.

Note: *A movie, a semester, a game, a party, etc. can be over, but a person cannot be over. You cannot say "I'm over." Instead, say "I'm finished."*

10. týpe/dó *something* óver (again) = redo; do something a second time

—I lost my homework, so I have to **do it over.**

Note: For emphasis, you can do something **all** over again.

11. táke a náp = sleep for a short time

S1: What time is it?
S2: About 2:00, I think. Why?
S1: I think I'll **take a nap** for a half hour or so. I can't keep my eyes open.

12. be únder préssure = have stress, tension, many responsibilities

S1: Modern women **are under** a lot of **pressure.** Many of them have to work, go to school, and take care of their families.
S2: I like the old days when women just stayed home.
S1: You're kidding. Really?

13. You can say thát again! = I agree with you completely.

S1: That test was really long.
S2: **You can say that again!** I needed another hour.

14. hít the bóoks = study (informal)

—Sorry I can't talk now. I have to **hit the books.**

15. táke a tést cóld = take a test without studying for it

S1: I can't believe I got an A!
S2: Why?
S1: I **took the test cold.**

■ *Exercises*

1. Mini-Dialogues

Below are two columns, A and B. Column A contains the first lines of dialogues and column B contains possible responses. For each opening line in column A, choose the *best* response from column B.

When checking this exercise in class, perform each mini-dialogue. One student should read an item from column A and another student should respond with the answer from column B.

A	B
_____ **1.** Uh-oh! I forgot to pick her up from the airport.	**a.** That's good, because she's been under a lot of pressure.
_____ **2.** I can't keep my eyes open.	**b.** Sorry. I didn't know.
_____ **3.** Want to get some coffee when class is over?	**c.** There's always a first time.
_____ **4.** If you don't hit the books a little more, you'll be sorry.	**d.** Sorry. I need to sleep.
_____ **5.** Can you do this over? I can't read it.	**e.** Oh no! Not again.
_____ **6.** She's on vacation.	**f.** Boy, you're going to be in hot water when she sees you.
_____ **7.** Ssh! The baby's taking a nap.	**g.** I can't find it. Can I have another one?
_____ **8.** I've never taken a test cold.	**h.** You can say that again!
_____ **9.** Let's pull an all-nighter together.	**i.** Why don't you take a nap?
_____ **10.** English is a crazy language.	**j.** You're right. I'll try to work harder.
_____ **11.** I was so nervous that my mind went blank.	**k.** So do I. That's the problem with cramming.
_____ **12.** You know, in some countries, people "do" a test.	**l.** For how long? The whole test?
_____ **13.** I ran all the way. Am I late?	**m.** No. You're lucky. You got here in the nick of time.
_____ **14.** After I cram for a test, I forget everything I studied.	**n.** Sounds like a good idea.
_____ **15.** Take out a piece of paper for a pop quiz.	**o.** Sure. I'll bring it in tomorrow.
_____ **16.** I'd like you to take out the handout I gave you yesterday.	**p.** I know. But in English it's "take."

2. Choosing the Idiom

The following dialogue takes place between the two people in the illustration. Fill in the blanks with some of the expressions on the list. Pay special attention to how the expressions are used grammatically. (You will need to consider verb tenses, subject-verb agreement, plurals, etc.) After you have checked your answers, perform the dialogue with a partner.

be under a lot of pressure   hit the books   get_____ sleep
be over   hand back   do over
pull an all-nighter   hand_____ in   take a nap
in the nick of time   cram   be in hot water

ALAN: What time is it?

CHARLIE: You don't want to know . . . It's 4:20.

ALAN: I need to _____ .
                              (1)

CHARLIE: No you don't. Just get another cup of coffee.

ALAN: I wish I had _____ every night. Then I
                              (2)

           wouldn't have to _____ now. I still have a
                                      (3)

           hundred pages to read.

CHARLIE: A hundred? We'd better stop talking. And I have to keep writing if I want

to _____ by 10:00.
(4)

ALAN: Let's take a five-minute break. I need to talk so I won't fall asleep . . . Don't

you think that students today _____ ? We're
(5)

each taking five classes and working in the bookstore and . . .

CHARLIE: So, what are you going to do? If you take fewer classes, it will take longer

to graduate. Listen, I'd really like to talk, but I'm going

to _____ if I don't get this paper finished.
(6)

ALAN: OK. I'm going to _____ . I'm setting my alarm
(7)

for 5:30. Wake me if I don't get up, OK? I'm not like you. I

can't _____ like you can.
(8)

3. Dictation

Your teacher or one of your classmates will read the dictation for this unit from Appendix A, or you will listen to the dictation on the audio program. You will hear the dictation three times. First, just listen. Second, as you listen, write the dictation on a separate sheet of paper. Third, as you listen, check what you have written.

4. Any Questions?

Take out a piece of paper. Do NOT write your name on it. On one side of the paper, write down what you think is the most interesting information that you have learned in this lesson up to now. On the other side of the paper, write down any questions that you have about any of the idioms. Your teacher will collect this paper and then answer your questions the next time you meet.

5. Personal Questions

Answer the questions below in a conversation with a partner or in a small group.

1. Have you ever pulled an all-nighter? If yes, where? When? What class was it for? What did you do to stay awake? If no, why not?

2. What kind of study habits do you (or did you) have as a student? That is, do you hit the books every night or do you cram at the last minute?

3. About tests: (a) Have you ever taken a test cold? If yes, explain the situation. (b) Has your mind ever gone blank during a test? If yes, explain what happened. (c) In your native country, do teachers give pop quizzes? What is your opinion of pop quizzes?

4. In your native country, can students turn in their work late? If they turn their work in late, what is the penalty? That is, do they get a lower grade?

5. Most people are under some kind of pressure. What kind of pressure are you under now?

6. Describe a situation in which you were in hot water. What happened?

6. Skit Writing

In this illustration, Alan and Charlie are in the cafeteria of their dormitory. It is the day after they pulled an all-nighter, and they are exhausted. They are telling their friends about the all-nighter, their tests and papers, and all the pressure they are under. Their friends tell them about their problems, too.

Work individually, in pairs, or as a class to write their conversation. Try to use at least five new expressions from this lesson and two expressions from previous lessons. After you have finished, perform the "skit" you created for your class.

7. Improvisation

Using the new expressions from this lesson, act out the following role-play. The new expressions should be written on the board.

You and your friends are studying for a big idiom test. It is 11 pm. Your teacher is going to test you on *every single idiom* in this book, so you can't go to sleep yet. You are all very tired and try to keep each other awake. One of you is testing the others.

Possible starting line:
Uh-oh! Your eyes are starting to close. Here—have some more coffee.

8. Real Life

Think of situations in your own life in which you might use some of the expressions from this lesson. Write down at least five. Outside of class, remember your list and try to use some of your new vocabulary. Also, when you watch TV and listen to people speak, listen carefully—you may hear these expressions.

Expressions	Real-Life Situations
Example: *in the nick of time*	*I would say this if I arrived at a bus stop or train station just when the bus or train arrived.*
1.	
2.	
3.	
4.	
5.	

Lesson 10

Sold Out

CLAIRE: **That's not fair!** Why didn't they **let us know** earlier? We've been **standing in line** for nothing! **What a waste of time!**

PAUL: No, it isn't. We can still **get into** the 11 o'clock show.

CLAIRE: I don't know if I'll be able to **stay up** so late. The 11 o'clock show doesn't **get out** until about 2 A.M.

PAUL: Well, if I know you, you can stay up for THIS show. Come on. Let's stay in line and get our tickets, and then **figure out** how to **kill** the **three hours.**

QUESTIONS
1. How would you react to such an announcement?
2. When you have to wait for something, what are some ways that you kill time?
3. In the United States, A.M. refers to the morning hours, and P.M. refers to the afternoon and evenings hours. Is the system the same or different in your native country? If it is different, what is the system?

■ Understanding the New Expressions

1. **be sóld oút** = no tickets or merchandise left

   S1: Did you get tickets to the basketball game?
   S2: No, there were no tickets left. In fact, the tickets have **been sold out**
   { for two weeks!
   { since last Sunday!
   S1: So, did you try to get some for the soccer game instead?
   S2: No, but that's a good idea. I hope that isn't **sold out,** too.

2. **be on sále/be for sále** = be available for people to buy
   will gó on sále = will (in the future) be available for people to buy

   S1: The newspaper says tickets for next week's football game **are on sale** now.
   S2: What are you waiting for? Let's go to the stadium right now. We can try to get tickets for next month's game, too.
   S1: No, those won't **go on sale** until Saturday.

   S1: Look! Bill's house **is for sale!**
   S2: I didn't know that he wanted to move.

   Contrast: **be ón sále** = be for sale at a reduced price

   S1: I think I'll buy that VCR that I saw last week.
   S2: Isn't it too expensive?
   S1: It was, but it**'s on sale** now. I can get it at half price.

3. **on a fírst-come, fírst-served básis** = the first people who arrive will be the first people served

   S1: Are the seats reserved?
   S1: No. Sorry. Seating is on a **first-come, first-served basis.**

   Similar expression: **first-cóme, first-sérved** (less formal)

   S1: OK, everyone. Dinner is ready. **First-come, first-served!**
   S2: Great! I'm starving.

4. **Thát's not fáir!**

   S1: I'd like you to wash the dishes tonight.
   S2: But I've washed the dishes every night this week. **That's not fair!**

   S1: The test had a lot of words on it that we never studied.
   S2: I know. **That** really **wasn't fair!**

Sold Out

5. lét *someone* knów = inform someone

S1: What time can you pick me up?
S2: I'm not sure. I'll **let** you **know** later.

S1: Good-bye. I'll miss you all.
S2: Write to us and **let** us **know** where you're staying.

S1: Thanks for helping me move into my new apartment.
S2: You're very welcome. **Let** me **know** if you need any more help.

6. stánd in líne = stay in a line of people until it is your turn to be served

S1: I got to the bank early so I wouldn't have to **stand in line.** But look at all these people!
S2: There are always lines here. I **stood in line** for half an hour last week.

Note: In some parts of the United States, people say "stand **on** line."

7. be a wáste of *something* = not a good use of, for example, time or money

S1: Standing in line **is a waste of** time.
S2: Next time let's bring books to read while we're waiting.

Similar expressions:

      (*to*) wáste (*something*) on (*something or someone*)

S1: Is that a good movie?
S2: No, it's awful. Don't **waste** your money **on** it.

      (*to*) wáste tíme (*doing something*)

S1: I drove to work today and it took me two hours.
S2: Why **waste time** driv**ing** in heavy traffic? You should take the train.

      (*to*) wáste (*something*)

S1: I don't believe you're going to finish that huge sandwich!
S2: I can't stand **to waste** food.

8. gét ínto (*a place*) gét ín = be allowed to enter

S1: I mailed my application. I hope I can **get into** the university.
S2: I know you'll be disappointed if you don't **get in.**

Similar expressions: **get someone ín/ínto** = use connections to help someone enter a place

S1: We're going to have to stand in line for the opening of the art exhibit.
S2: I know the director of the museum. Maybe he can { **get** us **in** early.
                                                    { **get** us **into** the museum
    early.

9. stáy úp (*inseparable/intransitive*) (+ ***gerund or infinitive***) = stay awake; not go to bed

S1: You just woke up? It's noon!
S2: I **stayed up** late last night { watching TV.
                                       { to watch TV.

10. gét oút (*inseparable/intransitive*) = leave when an activity such as a class or movie is finished

S1: Classes start at 9:00 and end at 3:00.
S2: You mean we won't **get out** until 3:00?

Similar expressions:

      gét óut of (*a place*)

S1: Let's **get out of** the house for a while.
S2: Good idea. I need some fresh air.

get (*someone or something*) óut (of) (a place)

S1: Please get that dog **out of** here!
S2: I'm **getting** him **out** right now.

11. fígure oút (*separable/transitive*)

S1: We're having a lot of trouble with this project.
S2: Let me help you **figure out** what to do. (= decide/determine)

S1: This is a really difficult problem. I can't **figure** it **out.** (= understand)
S2: Neither can I. Let's ask the teacher to explain it to us.

S1: What? Joe sold his car last night?
S2: Uh-huh. I can't **figure out** why he did it. (= understand)

S1: How do you like your new boss?
S2: She's very moody. I can't **figure** her **out.** (= understand)

12. kíll (*tíme*) (by) = do an activity to help the time pass

S1: We're early. What should we do now?
S2: We can **kill time by** playing cards.

S1: Oh, no! The flight has been delayed.
S2: Let's think of something to do to **kill the two hours.**

Similar expression: háve (*tíme*) to kíll

S1: We **have two hours to kill.** What do you want to do?
S2: Well, we can tell each other stories.

1. Mini-Dialogues

Below are two columns, A and B. Column A contains the first lines of dialogues and column B contains possible responses. For each opening line in column A, choose the *best* response from column B.

When checking this exercise in class, perform each mini-dialogue. One student should read an item from column A and another student should respond with the answer from column B.

A	B
_____ **1.** Uh-oh! They are sold out!	**a.** They'll let him know next week.
_____ **2.** The tickets went on sale last week.	**b.** That's too bad. They missed a good show.
_____ **3.** I bought this T-shirt for $40 on sale.	**c.** That's not fair! We were here first.
_____ **4.** We'd better get to the theater early.	**d.** But I needed to take a break.
_____ **5.** Those people are already being served.	**e.** Check the manual.
_____ **6.** Can you come over on Saturday night?	**f.** I know what you mean. It's a waste of time.
_____ **7.** When will he find out if he got the job?	**g.** Do you think it was a waste of money?
_____ **8.** I hate standing in line.	**h.** That's OK. We can get tickets for the next show.
_____ **9.** My car was cheap, but it has no power.	**i.** And we're wasting gas, too.
_____ **10.** Why aren't you studying? You're wasting time watching TV.	**j.** He's not easy to understand.
_____ **11.** We're lost. We've been driving around in circles.	**k.** And they're already sold out?
_____ **12.** They couldn't get into the concert so they went out to dinner.	**l.** She says she has the flu.
_____ **13.** How late did you stay up on New Year's Eve?	**m.** I'm not sure yet. I'll let you know.
_____ **14.** Why won't she get out of bed?	**n.** Good idea. Seating's first-come, first-served, isn't it?
_____ **15.** How did he get out of jail?	**o.** His uncle got him out.
_____ **16.** I can't figure out how to use this computer.	**p.** I guess we can kill time by playing a game of cards.
_____ **17.** He says one thing and does another. I can't figure him out.	**q.** What a bargain!
_____ **18.** We're early again. What should we do?	**r.** All night long.

2. Choosing the Idiom

The following dialogue takes place between the two people in the illustration. Fill in the blanks with some of the expressions on the list. Pay special attention to how the expressions are used grammatically. (You will need to consider verb tenses, subject-verb agreement, plurals, etc.) After you have checked your answers, perform the dialogue with a partner.

be sold out   stand in line
be on sale   get in
go on sale   get into
first-come, first-served   stay up
that's not fair   get out (of)
let (someone) know   figure (someone) out
a waste of (time) (money)   kill time
waste   have time to kill

DAN: How was the concert?

JEFF: We didn't _____ .
                          (1)

DAN: You're kidding! I thought you _____ for ten hours.
                                              (2)

JEFF: We did, but the tickets _____ before we got to
                                        (3)

the front of the line. It was awful. We _____ ten
                                                  (4)

hours standing in line.

112   Lesson 10

DAN: Standing?

JEFF: Well, we did sit down for awhile. We _____(5)_____ by

listening to music and sleeping.

DAN: Sleeping?

JEFF: Well, you know it was the middle of the night when we got there. I

couldn't _____(6)_____ .

DAN: Did you have a sleeping bag?

JEFF: Yes. Luckily, I had just bought a really good one

that _____(7)_____ for only $35.

DAN: That was lucky! Are you going to try to _____(8)_____ the

next concert?

JEFF: Of course! Tickets will _____(9)_____ on Saturday at 10:00

A.M., and I'm planning to be there starting Friday morning.

DAN: I can't _____(10)_____ . You're crazy!

JEFF: Maybe I am. But I love that music. And it's vacation now, so

I _____(11)_____ .

DAN: Are you sure you'll get tickets?

JEFF: I'd better! Tickets are sold _____(12)_____ , and I plan to

be the first one in line! Do you want to come to that concert with me?

DAN: Sure, if you stand in line for me.

JEFF: _____(13)_____ ! You have to stand in line with me. Come

on! It's fun!

DAN: I'm not sure right now. I'll _____(14)_____ .

Sold Out

113

3. Dictation

Your teacher or one of your classmates will read the dictation for this unit from Appendix A, or you will listen to the dictation on the audio program. You will hear the dictation three times. First, just listen. Second, as you listen, write the dictation on a separate sheet of paper. Third, as you listen, check what you have written.

4. Any Questions?

Take out a piece of paper. Do NOT write your name on it. On one side of the paper, write down what you think is the most interesting information that you have learned in this lesson up to now. On the other side of the paper, write down any questions that you have about any of the idioms. Your teacher will collect this paper and then answer your questions the next time you meet.

5. Personal Questions

Answer the questions below in a conversation with a partner or in a small group.

1. Can you think of an event—a concert, a game, a movie—that you couldn't go to because it was sold out? If yes, what event was it, how did you feel, and what did you do?

2. In what places do people typically stand in line in your native country? Are people generally polite, or do they push? Is it common for strangers in line to talk to each other?

3. What are some things that you do to kill time?

4. What are some things that you think people shouldn't waste? Why?

5. How late do you usually stay up? When you stay up late at night, do you need to sleep late the next morning?

6. Skit Writing

In this illustration, people are standing in line, waiting to buy tickets for Olympic events. Tickets will go on sale in five hours, and two people are talking about the events that they hope will not be sold out. They are bored.

Work individually, in pairs, or as a class to write their conversation. Try to use at least five new expressions from this lesson and two expressions from previous lessons. After you have finished, perform the "skit" you created for your class.

7. Improvisation

Using the new expressions from this lesson, act out the following role-play. The new expressions should be written on the board.

You and a few of your friends have "general admission" tickets for a special concert. General admission means that your tickets don't have seat numbers, so you are in line early in order to get the best possible seats. You are talking to your friends about how you can kill time in line, when suddenly a man who works at the theater walks over to the two people in front of you. The man takes the two people directly to the front of the line so that they will be able to enter the theater first. You and your friends are shocked.

Possible starting lines:
Does anyone have a deck of cards?

or

I'm tired of standing. Let's sit down and . . .

8. Real Life

Think of situations in your own life in which you might use some of the expressions from this lesson. Write down at least five. Outside of class, remember your list and try to use some of your new vocabulary. Also, when you watch TV and listen to people speak, listen carefully—you may hear these expressions.

Expressions	*Real-Life Situations*
Example: *That's not fair!*	*Children say this when they get a smaller piece of cake than other people*
1.	
2.	
3.	
4.	
5.	

Don't Throw it Away— Recycle!

DAVE: **Hold it,** Kathy! **What in the world** are you doing? **I can't believe my eyes!**

KATHY: What are you talking about?

DAVE: Don't you recycle? How can you **throw** glass **away?**

KATHY: Don't **get** so **upset,** Dave. I was only trying to . . .

LEE: She's right, Dave. **Take it easy.**

DAVE: OK, but I **can't get over** you. I thought you **cared about** the environment and . . .

KATHY: I *do* care, but there's no place to recycle bottles here, and I wanted to help **clean up.** You make me **feel** so **guilty.**

DAVE: I'm sorry. I did go a little crazy, but I **couldn't help it.** It's just that I've been **doing** some **research on** pollution, and I've **found out** that we're **running out of** places to put our garbage.

LEE: Listen, why don't we all **go through** these bags and **take** the bottles **out.** I'll take them home and recycle them.

DAVE: Are you sure it's no trouble? Because I can . . .

LEE: . . . no problem at all. They **pick up** newspaper, bottles, and cans **once a week** in my neighborhood. We've got a good recycling program.

KATHY: Well, let's **roll up our sleeves and get to work.**

DAVE: Ugh! What's in this bag???

QUESTIONS
1. Why is Dave upset with Kathy? Would *you* be upset with her? Why?
2. Do you think that Kathy should feel guilty?
3. Do you think that Lee agrees with Dave? Why or why not?
4. Do you recycle? If yes, what? (glass, paper, metal, plastic?)

■ Understanding the New Expressions

1. Hóld it! = Wait! Stop!

S1: This refrigerator sure is heavy. Walk very slowly.
S2: OK. Let's go.
S1: **Hold it** for a second. I have to move my hand.
S2: Are you OK now?
S1: Yeah, ready!

Note: *This expression does not mean that someone is holding something. It is often used in an urgent situation to ask someone to stop or wait. It can also be used in a situation that is not urgent, as you can see in the following:*

—Hey, you guys. **Hold it.** We're coming, too.

2. Whát in the wórld? = **Whát on éarth?** = What? (with real surprise/shock)

S1: What in the world are you doing here?
S2: I came to surprise you on your birthday.

Note: The question words (who, when, where, why, and how) can all be used in a similar way to show different strong feelings:

S1: Where in the world have you been? *(feelings: relief, anger)*
S2: I'm sorry I'm so late and that I made you worry. I got stuck in traffic.

—**What on earth** are you wearing? Those pants look fifty years old! *(surprise)*
—**Who on earth** could be calling us at 4:00 A.M.? *(surprise, anger, disbelief, fear)*
—**When on earth** will they get here? *(impatience, concern, anger)*
—**Why on earth** did they try to drive in this weather? *(concern, criticism)*
—**How on earth** can we get there by 8:00? It's already 7:30! *(concern, impatience)*

3. **I cán't belíeve my éyes!** = I can't believe what I'm looking at because I am very surprised.

   S1: I can't believe my eyes! Why did you dye your hair blond?
   S2: Relax. It's just a wig.

   Similar expression: **I cán't belíeve my éars!** = I can't believe what I hear because I am very surprised.

   S1: I can't believe my ears! Six months ago, you couldn't speak a word of English. You've certainly learned a lot!
   S2: Thanks. I study a lot, and my roommate helps me.

4. **thrów *something* awáy** = **thrów *something* óut** (separable/transitive) = put in the garbage (trash); dispose of

   S1: Ugh! Smell this cheese.
   S2: It must be two months old. **Throw** it **away.**

   S1: Where are my old jeans?
   S2: I **threw** them **out.**

   Contrast: **gét ríd of (*something*)** = put something in the garbage or give something to a person or place that needs what you don't want

   S1: I know that you want to **get rid of** those old clothes, but don't **throw** them **away.** Take them to a homeless shelter.
   S2: That's a great idea.

5. **gét upsét** = have your feelings go from being fine to disturbed because something bad happens

S1: Don't **get upset.** I told you that I'll come to the party. But I'll have to be a little late. I'll meet you there.

S2: I don't want to meet you there. I want to go together.

S1: You **get upset** so easily. This isn't such a big deal.

Similar Expression: **be upsét (with *someone* or about *something*):** after you *get* upset, you *are* upset

S1: I**'m** so **upset.**

S2: What's wrong?

S1: Everything was fine until I got my test back. I got a "C" and I thought I'd get an "A."

S1: I have to tell you that I**'m upset with** you.

S2: Oh, no. What did I do now?

S1: You promised you'd clean up before I got home, and people are coming over in five minutes. This place looks terrible.

S1: What **are** you **upset about?**

S2: Do you really want to know?

S1: I asked, didn't I?

S2: Well, I**'m upset about** a few things at work. One thing is that they keep giving me too much work and I'm always behind. Another thing is . . .

6. **Táke it éasy.** = Don't be upset; relax.

S1: I have so much work to do. I don't know how I can ever do it. I have to get this all done by Thursday, and . . .

S2: **Take it easy.** I'll help you. Tell me where to start.

S1: What are you going to do on Sunday?

S2: I'm just going to **take it easy.** I'll do some work in the garden and probably read for a while.

7. **cán't get óver *someone* or *something*** = can't believe something that happened because you are surprised

S1: I just got back yesterday, and I'm leaving again tomorrow.

S2: I **can't get over** you. You've become quite a traveler.

Don't Throw it Away—Recycle!

Note: *This expression is often used in the following ways to show surprise:*

—You cut your hair. I **can't get over** *how* different you look!

—I **can't get over** *who's* here—everyone from high school!

—I **can't get over** *what* she said to him. She let him know her feelings.

—I **can't get over** *where* they took us for dinner! It was so expensive.

—I **can't get over** *when* this work is due. We'll need at least another week to finish it.

—I **can't get over** *why* they got married. They don't love each other. They just want to live away from their families.

—I **can't get over** *how much* that costs. That's crazy. I won't buy it.

8. **cáre about** *someone or something* = have positive feelings for; be concerned about what happens to someone or something

S1: He **cares about** his family, but he wants to leave home and get his own apartment.
S2: Is there a problem?
S1: Yeah. His family doesn't understand.

S1: Why didn't you give him some money? Don't you **care about** the homeless?
S2: Sure I do. But I don't like giving money on the street.

S1: Do you **care about** politics? the environment? money?
S2: No. I don't **care about** all that. I just **care about** music.

Note: *A way very strongly (and not politely) to say, "I don't care" is to say either:* **I couldn't care less**, *or* **I could care less.**

Similar expression: **cáre for** *someone* = have positive feelings for a person (not a *thing*)

—He **cares for** his family, but he wants to leave home and get his own apartment.

S1. They **care for** each other, but they aren't ready to get married.
S2. They're smart to wait.

Note: *Care for* *is also used in formal eating situations such as in restaurants and at dinners where the hosts are formal. It means "want":*
S1: Would you **care for** some more? (= Would you like . . .?/ Do you *want* . . .?)
S2: Thanks. Just a little.

Contrast: **táke cáre (of)** = do what is necessary for someone or something

S1: Can you **take care of** the baby for a few hours so we can go to a movie?
S2: I'd be glad to. I hope he'll be awake so I can feed him and play with him.

S1: My car won't start and I don't know what to do.
S2: Take it easy. I'll **take care of** it.

S1: Bye. I'll see you in a few weeks. **Take care** (of yourself).
S2: I will. Bye.

9. **cléan úp (*something*)** (separable/transitive or intransitive) = clean completely after an event

S1: We can have a party in my house if everyone promises to help **clean up.**
S2: Everyone? Men, too?
S1: Uh-huh. Men, too.

S1: Did you have any damage from the earthquake?
S2: All the dishes fell out of the cabinets. It took us two weeks to **clean up** the kitchen. (Or: clean the kitchen up.)

Contrast: **to cléan** = make clean, usually on a regular basis

S1: We **clean** (vacuum, dust, wash the kitchen and bathroom floor) every Saturday morning.
S2: *Every week?* We **clean** only once a month.

10. **féel gúilty (about *something*)** = feel that something bad that happened was your responsibility

S1: My parents don't think that I write to them or call them enough. I didn't know that they felt that way and I **feel** kind of **guilty.**
S2: Well, write to them more often and then you won't have to **feel guilty.**

S1: I promised that I'd help her study on Sunday. I can't go to the beach.
S2: Just tell her that you don't feel well.
S1: I can't. I'd **feel** really **guilty about** lying.

Contrast: **be gúilty (of *something*)** = be the one who did something wrong, often in a legal sense

—She**'s guilty of** murder, but you can see from her face that she doesn't **feel guilty.**
—These two guys **are** not **guilty,** so stop asking them questions.

11. **cán't/cóuldn't hélp it**
cán't/cóuldn't hélp onesélf
cán't/cóuldn't help_____ ing *something* = do something because you can't control yourself

S1: You're eating too fast.
S2: I **can't help it.** I haven't eaten all day.

S1: You're eating too fast.
S2: I **can't help myself.** I haven't eaten all day.

S1: I **can't help** go**ing** shopping whenever there's a sale.
S2: Neither can I.

S1: I **couldn't help** tell**ing** him what I really thought.
S2: Is that why he's so upset?

12. **do résearch on (*a subject*)** = **to résearch** = carefully study something (often in a school) to gain information—("Research" can also be pronounced with the stress on the second syllable: reséarch)

> **S1:** Let's go get some coffee.
> **S2:** I can't. I have to go to the library.
> **S1:** Didn't you go yesterday?
> **S2:** Yes, but I'm **doing research on** the assassination of John Kennedy and some of the books that I need can't be taken out of the library. So I have to work there.

> **S1:** Excuse me. I'm **researching** what people do to improve their pronunciation. Can I ask you a few questions?
> **S2:** Sure.

13. **fínd óut** (usually inseparable) = get information

> **S1:** Have you seen my brother?
> **S2:** No. Why?
> **S1:** I have to **find out** what time (when) he's going to pick me up.

> **S1:** Where's the post office? I thought it was on this block.
> **S2:** So did I. Let's **find out** where it is.

> *Note:* *Find out can also be followed by* **who, why, how, how much, that,** *and* **about.** *Notice the word order. These are statements, not questions, so you should not say, "Let's find out where is the post office."*

—I need to **find out** *who* is doing research on John Kennedy.
—I'm trying to **find out** *why* he's been absent so long.
—Let's **find out** *how* to do this.
—We can't buy that until we **find out** *how much* it costs.
—When we **found out** *that* he was in the hospital, we called right away.
—We need to **find out** *about* it.
—We need to **find out** *where* the information desk is.

> *Note:* *When* **find out** *is separated, it is usually separated by the word, "that."*

> **S1:** Lisa's car was stolen last night.
> **S2:** How did you **find** *that* **out?**

> *Note:* *Find out is used only when talking about getting* **information.** *You can't say, "I can't find out where my car keys are" when you mean that you can't find your keys. Keys are not* **information.** *You should say, "I can't* **find** *my car keys."*

14. **rún óut (of *something*)** = have little or nothing of something left

> **S1:** If we don't find a gas station soon, we're going to **run out of** gas.
> **S2:** Why didn't you get gas before we left?

S1: We're **running out of** milk. Can you go to the store?
S2: In a minute. Let me finish this first.

S1: Where's Betty?
S2: We **ran out of** milk so she went to the store.

15. **gó thróugh** *something* = search/look for something that is mixed with other things; look at a collection of things so that you can take out what you don't want anymore.

S1: I can't find my paycheck.
S2: Did you look in your wallet?
S1: Three times. I **went through** everything, but my check wasn't there.

S1: Look at this! When I was cleaning, I was **going through** some old photos and found this baby picture.
S2: That's you? I can't believe it. You were really cute.

Note: *Some things that police might go through when they are searching for something are houses, cars, files, etc. Some things that you might go through when you are cleaning are old clothes, old school notes, books, and letters.*

Contrast: **gó thróugh** = have a difficult experience

Many families are **going through** hard times because of unemployment.
They **went through** a difficult divorce.

16. **táke** *something* **óut (of** *something*) = remove something from an enclosed area

S1: Where are my keys? They were in my pocket a minute ago.
S2: Maybe you **took** them **out of** your pocket when you were looking for change for the phone call.

S1: Hurry up! **Take** the letter **out of** the envelope! I can't wait.
S2: Calm down. I'll **take** it **out.**

Note: *You take something **out** of an enclosed area such as a bag, a drawer, a suitcase, a pocket, or an envelope. You take something **off** a space that is not enclosed such as a shelf or a table.*

Contrast: **táke** *someone* **óut (to)** = take someone to dinner, a movie, or other type of social outing and pay for that person

S1: I'd really like to **take you out to** dinner for your birthday. Are you free Saturday night?
S2: Oh, that's really nice. Thanks. I'm pretty sure I'm free.

Don't Throw it Away—Recycle!

17. pÍck Úp *something or someone* = go to a certain place to get something or someone

    S1: I have to **pick up** my books at Sandra's house, and then I'll come home.
    S2: After you **pick** them **up,** could you stop at the store for some bread?

    S1: Can you **pick** me **up** tomorrow if it rains?
    S2: Sure. No problem.

18. Ónce a wÉek = one time a week

    S1: How often to you go to your art class?
    S2: Just **once a week.**

    Note: *Once a week* and **twice a week** *(= two times a week) are common, but we say* **three times a week, four times a week,** *etc.*

    Note: *You can also say* **once a month, once a year, once a day, once in a while** *(= occasionally).*

19. rÓll up one's slÉeves and gÉt to wÓrk = get ready to do some (usually physical) work

    S1: You'd better stop reading the newspaper and **roll up your sleeves and get to work.** It's already one o'clock.
    S2: Just let me finish this article.

1. Mini-Dialogues

Below are two columns, A and B. Column A contains the first lines of dialogues and column B contains possible responses. For each opening line in column A, choose the *best* response from column B.

When checking this exercise in class, perform each mini-dialogue. One student should read an item from column A and another student should respond with the answer from column B.

A

_____ **1.** Hold it!

_____ **2.** I don't know what I'm going to do. I'm so worried.

_____ **3.** We've got a lot to do today.

_____ **4.** How often do you brush your teeth?

_____ **5.** What in the world is that?

_____ **6.** Where's the bag that was on the table?

_____ **7.** I can't get over how polluted the air is here. It smells terrible.

_____ **8.** I feel guilty about driving. It adds to the air pollution.

_____ **9.** I'm going to learn how to fly.

_____ **10.** I lost my ring. I'm going to go through everything in my room 'til I find it.

_____ **11.** Hey! Stop laughing!

_____ **12.** What happened when you told them that you lost it?

_____ **13.** I care about learning English, but sometimes I get a little lazy.

_____ **14.** OK, everybody. It's time to clean up. Put everything away.

_____ **15.** When should I take the cake out of the oven?

_____ **16.** My pen ran out of ink.

_____ **17.** I can't get over how beautiful your house is.

_____ **18.** Would you care for some coffee, sir?

B

a. My pet snake.

b. I can't believe my ears!

c. Uh-oh—I threw it away. Was it important?

d. Take it easy. We'll find out what you should do.

e. Everything? Good luck!

f. They got really upset.

g. So let's roll up our sleeves and get to work. I'm ready.

h. Here's a pencil.

i. Twice a day. How about you?

j. Yes, de-caf (decaffeinated), please.

k. I know. On really bad days, older people and sick people are told to stay in their houses.

l. I know what you mean. It's hard work.

m. Where should I put the paint?

n. I'm sorry—I can't help it—you look so funny.

o. Why don't you ride your bike?

p. Thanks. We just painted it.

q. In about a half hour.

r. Do you want to come with us?

2. Choosing the Idiom

The following dialogue takes place between the two people in the illustration. Fill in the blanks with some of the expressions on the list. Pay special attention to how the expressions are used grammatically. (You will need to consider verb tenses, subject-verb agreement, plurals, etc.) After you have checked your answers, perform the dialogue with a partner.

clean up	feel guilty	can't believe my eyes
take it easy	care for	can't get over
what in the world	get so upset	run out of
find out about	care about	can't help it

ANITA: _____ (1) is happening to the earth?

I _____ (2) .

PHILIP: What happened?

ANITA: There was another oil spill. There is oil covering miles of the ocean near the

coast. I just _____ (3) how often this has happened.

Isn't there anything they can do to prevent this kind of thing?

PHILIP: I have no idea. But you shouldn't _____ (4) .

_____ (5) !

ANITA: I _____(6)_____ . What kind of world will our children live

in? The forests are being cut down, we have air and water pollution,

we're _____(7)_____ places for our garbage. We need

to _____(8)_____ the earth to make it a healthier place.

PHILIP: You're absolutely right. But if you _____(9)_____ the earth

so much, why don't you do something about it?

ANITA: Are you trying to make me _____(10)_____ ?

PHILIP: No. I just think you should _____(11)_____ what you can

do to help. Why don't you call one of the environmental groups?

3. Dictation

Your teacher or one of your classmates will read the dictation for this unit from Appendix A, or you will listen to the dictation on the audio program. You will hear the dictation three times. First, just listen. Second, as you listen, write the dictation on a separate sheet of paper. Third, as you listen, check what you have written.

4. Any Questions?

Take out a piece of paper. Do NOT write your name on it. On one side of the paper, write down what you think is the most interesting information that you have learned in this lesson up to now. On the other side of the paper, write down any questions that you have about any of the idioms. Your teacher will collect this paper and then answer your questions the next time you meet.

5. Personal Questions

Answer the questions below in a conversation with a small group.

1. Before your discussion, make a list of all the environmental problems that you can think of. Then number the items on the list, with number one being the most serious problem and the highest number being the least serious problem.

Compare your list and your rankings with the lists and rankings of some of your classmates. Discuss how your lists are similar and different (and try to include some of the new idioms in your discussion). Then try to make one list that all members of your group agree on. You should all also agree on the rankings of the individual items.

Once this is done, it should be interesting for all the groups in your class to share and compare their lists.

2. What do you do to help take care of the earth? Do you: recycle, have a smog control device on your car (if you have a car), avoid throwing garbage out of car windows, avoid littering? What other things can you and other people do?

3. Are there recycling programs in your native country? If yes, what is recycled? Explain the recycling system.

4. Is there a recycling program in the place where you are studying English? If yes, try to find out more about it if you can. If no, would you want to start a program?

5. What kinds of things do your friends and relatives do that make you upset?

6. If you are invited to dinner at a friend's house, do you help clean up? Why or why not?

7. What is one thing about the English language that you can't get over?

8. What is one thing that you care a lot about? What is one thing that you don't care about at all?

9. Discuss some of the things students in your English program have to find out about before they first start classes.

6. Skit Writing

In this illustration, Barbara, Bill, and their two children are in their car in bumper-to-bumper traffic in an industrial area. On both sides of the highway they see oil refineries and smoke coming out of factories. Barbara and Bill feel upset about what they see and smell, and complain to each other.

Work individually, in pairs, or as a class to write their conversation. Try to use at least five new expressions from this lesson and two expressions from previous lessons. After you have finished, perform the "skit" you created for your class.

7. Improvisation

Using the new expressions from this lesson, act out the following role-play. The new expressions should be written on the board.

There has been a train derailment (a train went off its tracks), and a dangerous chemical is leaking into the air near your neighborhood. You and your neighbors have been evacuated to a high school gym (gymnasium), where the air is safe. You will all stay there for at least one night while government officials and scientists try to find out how dangerous the situation is and what needs to be done.

A group of you in the gym talk about how dangerous the world has become. Naturally, you are all very upset and want to express your feelings. Luckily, there are some people in the group who try to get the others to calm down and take it easy.

Possible starting line:
I can't believe that this happened to us!

8. Real Life

Think of situations in your own life in which you might use some of the expressions from this lesson. Write down at least five. Outside of class, remember your list and try to use some of your new vocabulary. Also, when you watch TV and listen to people speak, listen carefully—you may hear these expressions.

Expressions	*Real-Life Situations*
Example: *pick up*	*I would say that I have to pick up my kids from school in the afternoon.*

1.

2.

3.

4.

5.

Let's Make a Toast

HIROSHI: **Quiet down,** everyone. I'd like to **make a toast to** our class. **May you** all be healthy, happy, and successful in your lives. And successful with your English.

MARIA: **I'll drink to that!** And I'd like to make another toast. This one is to our teacher. Thank you for **bending over backwards** to explain this crazy language to us. You patiently **put up with** our questions, and we always knew that we could **count on** you to **give us a hand** when we needed help.

TEACHER: Thanks, everyone. And now I'd like to make a toast to you. I'll miss you, your questions, and your wonderful **sense of humor. I wish you the best,** and I hope that you'll all keep in touch with each other, and with me.

HIROSHI: We will, **no matter what.**

1. What do you say in your native language when you make a toast? What does it mean in English?
2. On what occasions do you make toasts in your native country?

■ Understanding the New Expressions

1. **qúiet dówn** = *be quiet* (but "quiet down" is more polite)

   S1: Can you help me get the attention of the audience?
   S2: Sure. **Quiet down,** please! We'd like to make an announcement.

   Note: The word "please" along with a friendly tone of voice makes "quiet down" more polite.

   qúiet (*someone*) dówn = get someone to make less noise

   S1: The children are much too noisy. We can't begin.
   S2: I'm going to **quiet** them **down** so that we can start the show.

2. **máke a tóast (to)** = express good wishes while holding up a drink

   S1: I'd like to **make a toast.** We all wish you many years of happiness.
   S2: Thank you. And we'd like to **make a toast to** all our wonderful friends. Thank you for celebrating with us today.

   Note: Don't forget "a". If you say, "I want to make toast," you mean that you want to cook bread!

   Similar expressions:

   Hére's to *someone or something*

   S1: Here's to Mom and Dad. Happy anniversary!
   S2: This is such a wonderful surprise! Thank you.

S1: **Here's to** success at your new job!
S2: Thanks.

Chéers!

S1: I'm so glad we could get together for a drink.
S2: So am I. **Cheers!**

3. **may you/may we/may they** = an opening phrase of a toast

S1: **May you** always be healthy and happy.
S2: And **may we** always be friends.

4. **I'll drínk to thát!** = a response to a toast that you agree with

S1: Here's to a great vacation!
S2: **I'll drink to that!**

5. **beńd over báckwards (to)** = try very hard (PAST = bent)

S1: Did you finish painting the house last weekend?
S2: Yes, thanks to my brother. He **bent over backwards to** help us.

6. **pút úp with** *someone or something* *(cannot be separated)* = tolerate

S1: How do you **put up with** your noisy roommates?
S2: It's hard, but I like them a lot.

S1: I'm anxious to get back home. I can't **put up with** this cold weather.
S2: Lucky you. I wish I were going with you.

7. **cóunt on** *someone or something* **(to)** *(inseparable/transitive)* = depend on

S1: Thanks for giving me the chance to do this job. I hope I can do it well.
S2: I know you can do it. And if you have any problems, you can **count on** me **to** help you.

S1: What else do we need to pack for our trip?
S2: We can't **count on** good weather, so we'd better take raincoats.

8. **gíve** *someone* **a hánd (with)** = help someone

S1: Let me **give** you **a hand with** those suitcases.
S2: Thanks. They're really heavy.

S1: How did you carry all that?
S2: My friend **gave** me **a hand.**

Contrast: **gíve** *someone* **a hánd** = applaud, clap hands

S1: How was the jazz group at the Student Union?
S2: Terrific! The audience **gave** them **a big hand.**

9. **have a sénse of húmor** = have the ability to laugh and also to make jokes

S1: Did you have a good time with your old friend the other night?
S2: Yes. I couldn't stop laughing. She **has** such **a** great **sense of humor.**

10. **I wísh you the bést** = a formal way to express good wishes to someone

S1: **I wish you** all **the best.**
S2: And I wish the same for you.

11. **nó mátter whát** = nothing will stop the plans

S1: We're going to have a picnic Saturday, **no matter what.** I promise.
S2: What if it rains?
S1: Then we'll have the picnic on the porch.

S1: My plane doesn't get in until late. I'll wake you up when I get home.
S2: **No matter what** time you get here, I'll be awake. I can't wait to see you!

Contrast:

Whát's the mátter (with *someone or something*)? = What's wrong?

S1: **What's the matter** (with you)? Don't you feel well?
S2: I'm so tired, and I still haven't finished my homework.

It dóesn't mátter = It's not important

S1: I'm sorry I'm late.
S2: **It doesn't matter** because we still have time to get there.

1. **Mini-Dialogues**

Below are two columns, A and B. Column A contains the first lines of dialogues and column B contains possible responses. For each opening line in column A, choose the *best* response from column B.

When checking this exercise in class, perform each mini-dialogue. One student should read an item from column A and another student should respond with the answer from column B.

A

_____ 1. I'd like to make a toast to the new graduate. May she never have trouble finding a job!

_____ 2. Please quiet down.

_____ 3. I can't hear the TV because the kids are making so much noise.

_____ 4. Great speech! Let's give her a big hand!

_____ 5. Why are you so upset?

_____ 6. It's so hot here all the time. Do you like it?

_____ 7. Why did she leave so early?

_____ 8. You'll help me with my homework tonight, won't you?

_____ 9. Where are you going?

_____ 10. Can I give you a hand?

_____ 11. The jokes in that movie weren't so funny. Why were you laughing so much?

_____ 12. Bye, Chris. Have a good trip. I wish you the best. And remember to write.

B

a. Thanks, I really appreciate it.

b. She couldn't put up with the noise.

c. I will, no matter what.

d. I'll drink to that.

e. Not really, but I put up with it.

f. Sorry. I didn't realize we were being so noisy.

g. Bravo, Cindy! You did a great job!

h. I guess I have a strange sense of humor.

i. I'll try to quiet them down.

j. I bent over backwards to help them, but they didn't even thank me.

k. You can count on me.

l. To give them a hand with their homework.

2. Choosing the Idiom

The following conversation takes place among the three people in the illustration. Fill in the blanks with some of the expressions on the list. Pay special attention to how the expressions are used grammatically. (You will need to consider verb tenses, subject-verb agreement, plurals, etc.) After you have checked your answers, perform the conversation in groups of three.

bend over backwards
sense of humor
may you
may we
I'll drink to that
quiet down
make a toast
here's to

put up with
count on
I wish you the best
give (someone) a hand
no matter what
it doesn't matter
what's the matter

ASTRONAUT 1: _____ , everyone. It's time
                              (1)

to _____ to ourselves. We've now been
                    (2)

up here in space for 100 days. _____
                                              (3)

be up here for another 100!

ASTRONAUT 2: _____ !
                              (4)

ASTRONAUT 3:   I won't! I can't _____ this life any more.
                                          (5)

                I want to go home.

ASTRONAUT 2:   Why? _____ ? Are you homesick? We
                                    (6)

                have all _____ to make you happy
                                      (7)

                here. You have the best bed, good books to read, . . .

ASTRONAUT 3:   I know it, and I thank you. But I'm going to go back home

                soon, _____ .
                                  (8)

ASTRONAUT 1:   How are you going to get there?

ASTRONAUT 3:   With the supply ship. The guy on the supply ship told me that I could

                go with him next time if I _____
                                                      (9)

                with his work.

ASTRONAUT 1:   When did he say he would be here again?

ASTRONAUT 3:   In two weeks.

ASTRONAUT 1:   Ha! Two weeks? He probably won't be back for two months!

ASTRONAUT 3:   That's not very funny!

ASTRONAUT 1:   You have no _____ .
                                        (20)

ASTRONAUT 3:   I know he'll be here in two weeks. That's what he told me, and I

                am _____ him to come.
                                (11)

ASTRONAUT 2:   And if he doesn't, what will you do?

3. Dictation

Your teacher or one of your classmates will read the dictation for this unit from Appendix A, or you will listen to the dictation on the audio program. You will hear the dictation three times. First, just listen. Second, as you listen, write the dictation on a separate sheet of paper. Third, as you listen, check what you have written.

4. Any Questions?

Take out a piece of paper. Do NOT write your name on it. On one side of the paper, write down what you think is the most interesting information that you have learned in this lesson up to now. On the other side of the paper, write down any questions that you have about any of the idioms. Your teacher will collect this paper and then answer your questions the next time you meet.

5. Personal Questions

Answer the questions below in a conversation with a partner or in a small group.

1. What would you like to say to your classmates and teacher when your class ends? Make up toasts for your teacher and at least three students who are not in your group.

Start with: "To _____ . May you _____ ."

You can add: "I'll (or we'll) always remember you for _____ ."

For example: "To Kim. May you become completely fluent in English as soon as possible. We'll always remember your great acting in our role-plays."

2. Do you think you have a good sense of humor? Is it hard for someone to make you laugh? Why or why not? Do you like to tell jokes?

3. What is something that you bent over backwards to do and succeeded in doing?

4. Describe a friend or relative of yours whom you can always count on.

6. Skit Writing

In this illustration, Suzanne and Larry have just gotten married, and they are at their wedding reception. Their friend, Alex, is making a toast to them. After the toast, Alex asks Larry if Suzanne can count on him to share the housework because Suzanne won't put up with doing it all. She believes in sharing the work "50–50."

Work individually, in pairs, or as a class to write their conversation: first, the toast, and then the jokes about housework. Try to use at least five new expressions from this lesson and two expressions from previous lessons. After you have finished, perform the "skit" you created for your class.

7. Improvisation

Using the new expressions from this lesson, act out the following role-play. The new expressions should be written on the board.

Members of your group have just:

(a) won the lottery
(b) gotten engaged or married
(c) graduated
(d) had a baby
(e) gotten a new job
(f) gotten out of jail
(g) bought a new house
(h) been elected to a high position
(i) _____ (situation of your choice)

You and your classmates celebrate this great occasion with toasts. Possible starting lines: I can't believe it!

or

I'd like to make a toast to ____.

8. Real Life

Think of situations in your own life in which you might use some of the expressions from this lesson. Write down at least five. Outside of class, remember your list and try to use some of your new vocabulary. Also, when you watch TV and listen to people speak, listen carefully—you may hear these expressions.

Expressions	*Real-Life Situations*
Example: *count on*	*I would tell my best friends and my relatives that they could always count on me to be there to help them*

1.

2.

3.

4.

5.

Crossword Puzzle

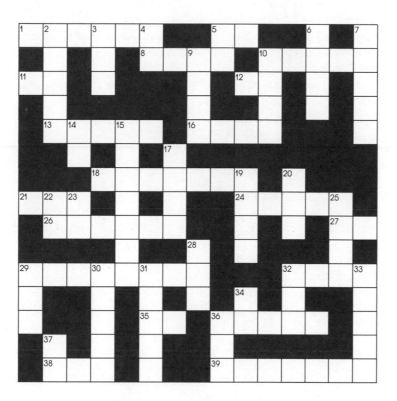

Across

1. I _____ an all-nighter again. I need to get some sleep.

5. I'm going to _____ in hot water if I don't take care of some business.

8. _____ a year we take a big trip.

10. You can _____ on me. I'll be glad to help you.

11. She _____ guilty. I know it.

12. We'll _____ over the test tomorrow.

13. I'll like to make a _____ . May we all stay in touch.

16. My _____ went blank during the test.

18. I can't _____ my ears—did you say that you were going to have a baby?

21. You can count on _____ to help you when you need help.

24. You can say that _____ .

26. Hurry up! First-come, first-_____ .

27. I don't want to stand _____ line.

29. Today, students are under a lot of _____ .

32. I didn't study at all, so I guess I'll have to _____ the test cold.

35. I lost my homework, so I have to _____ it over.

36. _____ to everyone in our class! May you all do whatever you want in your lives.

38. Ssh! The baby's taking a _____ .

39. We need to go _____ all of our notes to study for the final.

Down

2. What are you _____ about?
3. I'll _____ you know tomorrow.
4. I need to _____ some research in the library.
5. Everything in that store will _____ on sale tomorrow.
6. _____ in your homework at the end of class.
7. Yesterday we _____ in line for almost an hour.
9. Whenever I _____ for a test, I forget everything when the test is over.
10. I'm never going to take a test _____ again.
14. Let's get rid _____ all this junk.
15. We need to roll up our _____ and get to work right away.
17. same as 16 across
19. I can't believe my _____. What did you say?
20. _____ we all learn English as fast as we can.
22. She _____ in hot water with her mother.
23. Do you want _____ to help you clean up?
25. You got here in the _____ of time.
28. I need to _____ some sleep.
29. OK, everyone. Get ready for a _____ quiz.
30. He was trying to get some _____ in the park, but it was too noisy.
31. When you're not _____ pressure, you're so relaxed.
32. I started to hit _____ books at 11 last night.
33. Where on _____ have you been?
34. They can't _____ sold out! I can't believe it.
36. I'd better go. I have to _____ the books because I have a test tomorrow.
37. You can count _____ me.

Tic Tac Toe

In this variation of tic tac toe, to get an X or an O you must create a grammatically correct sentence that is logical in meaning. Here is a game to start you off. Create as many games as you like, using expressions from Lessons 9–12.

in the nick of time	do research	can't get over
give someone a hand	cram	put up with
why on earth	figure out	let someone know

Guess the Idiom

Look at these cartoons and try to guess which expressions from lessons 9–12 they represent.

1. _____

2. _____

3. _____

4. _____

5. _____

6. _____

Review Games for Lessons 9–12

Appendix A — Dictations

■ Lesson 1 — Cold Feet

Two weeks before they got married, Jana and Rick were in a swimming pool talking to their best friends. At one end of the pool, Jana was telling her friend, Ellen, that she was getting cold feet because they couldn't even afford to buy furniture. Ellen didn't use these exact words, but she basically told Jana that she could tell that deep down she loved Rick and that she shouldn't have second thoughts about getting married.

At the other end of the pool, Rick was telling his friend, Tim, that he was afraid of making a mistake, that marriage was for good, and that his parents were divorced and he didn't want history to repeat itself. Tim told Rick not to be so chicken and predicted that if Rick wound up without Jana, he would be very sorry.

■ Lesson 2 — Guess Who?

Two old friends, Laura and Pete, ran into each other at a restaurant. They hadn't seen each other in ages. Laura invited Pete to join her, but he was on his way to the city and had to get going right away because of the traffic. They agreed to drop in on each other sometime. The question is, will they really try to see each other again?

■ Lesson 3 — Please Leave a Message After You Hear the Beep

Melissa doesn't worry a lot, but she freezes when she has to talk on an answering machine. She gets tongue-tied and doesn't know what to say.

One day, when she made a call about renting an apartment, she heard the greeting, "Please leave a message after you hear the beep." When she heard this, she hung up and wrote down what she wanted to say. When she was just about ready to call back, Steve walked in. She told him about how afraid she was, and he offered to make the call for her. Melissa thanked him, but told him that she had to make the call on her own. She told him to have a seat and wish her luck, and then she took a deep breath and made the call.

■ Lesson 4 — In Bad Shape

Carmen and Nick are good friends, and Nick was worried when he noticed that Carmen was absent from school. He called her up and found out that she had caught a terrible cold. She said that she was in really bad shape. He had a cold, too, and told her that they were in the same boat. When she asked him to come over to keep her company, he told her that he couldn't stop sneezing and that he just wanted to go to bed.

■ Lesson 5 — Are We Couch Potatoes?

Andy and Susan got together with Ruth and Michael to watch some videotapes. They rented a tearjerker and a horror movie, and decided to watch the horror movie first because Ruth said she didn't feel like crying.

Michael is the kind of guy who doesn't think it's good to watch a lot of TV. He said that they spent too much time sitting on the couch, glued to the tube. He was worried about becoming a couch potato. His friends were surprised to hear this because Michael reads a lot. In fact, Susan called him a "bookworm."

■ Lesson 6 — Forgetting a Date

Bob stood Nancy up, and that was the beginning of a lot of trouble. When she got angry at him, he said that he was sorry for hurting her feelings, and he offered to treat her to dinner to make up for hurting her. But that wasn't enough. Nancy wanted to know what had really happened, and Bob finally told her that he had taken his old girlfriend to dinner. Naturally, Nancy was upset, but they made up. They made plans to go to the movies that night at 7.

Nancy waited and waited for Bob to show up that evening. He didn't come. She thought that he was standing her up again, but he wasn't. Something terrible had happened.

Lesson 7 — For Here or to Go?

Mollie and Ronnie were standing in line at a fast-food restaurant when someone cut in line in front of them. They decided not to say anything because they didn't want any trouble.

When Mollie told Ronnie that lunch was on her, he first told her that he wanted to treat her.

When she said no, he suggested that they split the check. She still said no, so she won—she treated him to lunch.

While they were eating, they were talking about their friend, Casey, who was taking a class to help him stop smoking. They were surprised when Casey walked in. He sat down and told them that he was doing pretty well so far and that he had promised himself that he wouldn't end up being the only smoker in town.

Lesson 8 — How About Going to a Movie?

One morning, Rosemary was practicing standing on her head when the telephone rang. It was Frank, a guy who really liked her. She liked him, too, but just as a friend. He asked her if she could go to the movies, but she said she had to take a rain check because she had a lot of homework. He told her to take some time off because she studied so much that she would turn into a robot. Finally, he talked her into going out when he told her that it was his birthday.

Lesson 9 — Pulling an All-Nighter

Annette is under a lot of pressure at school. Last night she pulled an all-nighter writing a report, and she finished it in the nick of time. Then, in the morning, when she had a pop quiz, her mind went blank. Her friend, Alan, told her to take a nap in the afternoon, but Annette explained that she couldn't because she had to study for another test. It seems that Annette needs to organize her time better so that she won't have to do everything at the last minute.

Lesson 10 — Sold Out

Paul and Claire were standing in line to buy tickets to a show they really wanted to see. They were surprised when it was announced that the 8 o'clock show was sold out. Paul wanted to get tickets for the 11 o'clock show, but Claire was afraid that she wouldn't be able to stay up that late. He disagreed, and told her that she would be able to stay up because she really wanted to see the show. Paul suggested that while they were standing in line, they should try to figure out how they could kill the next three hours.

■ Lesson 11 — Don't Throw It Away—Recycle

A school club had a meeting and then a party one evening. After the party, only Dave, Kathy, and Lee were left because they were the "Clean-up Committee." They were all cleaning when Dave suddenly noticed that Kathy was throwing a glass bottle away. He got really upset because she wasn't recycling. He told her that he couldn't get over her and she told him that he made her feel guilty.

Lee interrupted and suggested that they all go through the garbage bags and take out the bottles. She said that she would take the bottles home and recycle them.

While they were doing this, they decided to start a recycling program for bottles, cans, and paper in their school.

■ Lesson 12 — Let's Make a Toast

At their last English class, some people made toasts. Hiroshi made a toast to the class, wishing the students healthy, happy, and successful lives. Maria said that she would drink to that and then made a toast to their teacher. She thanked him for bending over backwards to explain English and for putting up with their many questions. She told him that everyone knew that they could count on him for his help. The teacher thanked her and then made a toast to the whole class. He told them that he would miss them, their questions, and their wonderful sense of humor. He wished them the best and said that he hoped they would all keep in touch.

Appendix B —
Answer Key

■ Lesson 1 — Cold Feet

Exercise 1

1. o
2. c
3. j
4. h
5. k
6. a
7. p
8. d
9. b
10. g
11. e
12. l
13. n
14. m
15. i
16. q
17. f

Exercise 2

1. cold feet *or* second thoughts
2. don't have second thoughts *or* don't have cold feet
3. can tell
4. am dying to
5. get married
6. have a lot in common
7. deep down
8. through (with)

■ Lesson 2 — Guess Who?

Exercise 1

1.	j (or b)	7.	a
2.	h	8.	i
3.	k	9.	d
4.	l	10.	e
5.	f	11.	c
6.	b	12.	g

Exercise 2

1. run into
2. in ages
3. Come on
4. get going
5. out of the way *or* out of my way
6. drop in
7. out of touch
8. feel free to

■ Lesson 3 — Please Leave a Message After You Hear the Beep

Exercise 1

1.	e	8.	b
2.	i	9.	h
3.	k	10.	j
4.	n	11.	l
5.	a	12.	d
6.	c	13.	m
7.	f	14.	g

Exercise 2

1. am going out of my mind
2. going on
3. call back
4. was just about ready
5. hang up
6. a busy signal
7. Sorry, I have another call. Can you hold on

■ Lesson 4 — In Bad Shape

Exercise 1

1.	f	9.	a
2.	h	10.	e
3.	l	11.	m
4.	n	12.	o
5.	i	13.	d
6.	g	14.	p
7.	j	15.	q
8.	c	16.	b

Exercise 2

1. all night long
2. can't stop
3. sounds like
4. take his temperature
5. feel sorry for
6. Chances are
7. get over
8. are in the same boat
9. are in good shape *or* got over it
10. What do you mean
11. keep me company
12. I have news for you

■ Lesson 5 — Are We Couch Potatoes?

Exercise 1

1.	h	8.	j
2.	k	9.	c
3.	d	10.	m
4.	i	11.	f
5.	e	12.	l
6.	a	13.	n
7.	b	14.	g

Exercise 2

1. feel like
2. a couch potato
3. spend all my time
4. How about
5. in the mood
6. That makes two of us
7. You're kidding
8. scares me out of my wits
9. That's funny

■ Lesson 6 — Forgetting a Date

Exercise 1

1.	e	8.	g
2.	h	9.	f
3.	b	10.	k
4.	j	11.	i
5.	a	12.	m
6.	d	13.	l
7.	c		

Exercise 2

1. making up
2. To be honest with you
3. make up
4. stood me up
5. stand for
6. can't stand
7. show up
8. treated her
9. hurt my feelings
10. work it out *or* make up
11. You've got a point there

■ Lesson 7 — For Here or to Go?

Exercise 1

1.	j	10.	o (or n)
2.	r	11.	e
3.	k	12.	m
4.	a	13.	n
5.	g	14.	q
6.	b	15.	l
7.	c	16.	f
8.	i	17.	p
9.	d	18.	h

Exercise 2

1. taking this class
2. made a promise
3. end up
4. figure
5. look who's here
6. how's it going?
7. So far, so good
8. eat out
9. It's on me

■ Lesson 8 — How About Going to a Movie?

Exercise 1

1. c
2. i
3. e
4. g
5. h
6. b
7. d
8. f
9. a

Exercise 2

1. turn you into
2. take a rain check
3. get . . . over with
4. give you a rain check
5. Make some time for
6. Before you know it
7. Take some time off
8. When you put it that way
9. change your mind
10. talked me into

■ Lesson 9 — Pulling an All-Nighter

Exercise 1

1. f
2. i
3. n
4. j
5. o
6. a
7. b
8. c
9. d
10. h
11. l
12. p
13. m
14. k
15. e
16. g

Exercise 2

1. get some sleep
2. hit the books
3. pull an all-nighter *or* cram
4. hand this in
5. are under a lot of pressure
6. be in hot water
7. take a nap
8. pull an all-nighter

■ Lesson 10 — Sold Out

Exercise 1

1.	h	10.	d
2.	k	11.	i
3.	q	12.	b
4.	n	13.	r
5.	c	14.	l
6.	m	15.	o
7.	a	16.	e
8.	f	17.	j
9.	g	18.	p

Exercise 2

1. get in
2. stood in line
3. were sold out
4. wasted
5. killed time
6. stay up
7. was on sale
8. get into
9. go on sale
10. figure you out
11. have time to kill *or* can kill time
12. first-come, first-served
13. That's not fair
14. let you know

■ Lesson 11 — Don't Throw it Away—Recycle

Exercise 1

1.	r	10.	e
2.	d	11.	n
3.	g	12.	f
4.	i	13.	l
5.	a	14.	m
6.	c	15.	q
7.	k	16.	h
8.	o	17.	p
9.	b	18.	j

Exercise 2

1. What in the world
2. can't believe my eyes
3. can't get over
4. get so upset
5. Take it easy
6. can't help it
7. running out of
8. clean up
9. care about
10. feel guilty
11. find out about

■ Lesson 12 — Let's Make a Toast

Exercise 1

1. d
2. f
3. i
4. g
5. j
6. e
7. b
8. k or c
9. l
10. a
11. h
12. c or k

Exercise 2

1. Quiet down
2. make a toast
3. May we
4. I'll drink to that
5. put up with
6. What's the matter (with you)
7. bent over backwards
8. no matter what
9. gave him a hand
10. sense of humor
11. counting on

Appendix C — Answer Key For Review Games

■ **Review Games for Lessons 1–4**

Crossword Puzzle

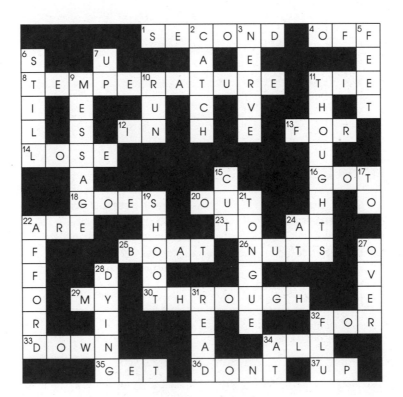

Guess the Idiom

1. have cold feet
2. tie the knot
3. go bananas
4. be off her rocker
5. be in the same boat
6. have a seat

■ Review Games for Lessons 5–8

Crossword Puzzle

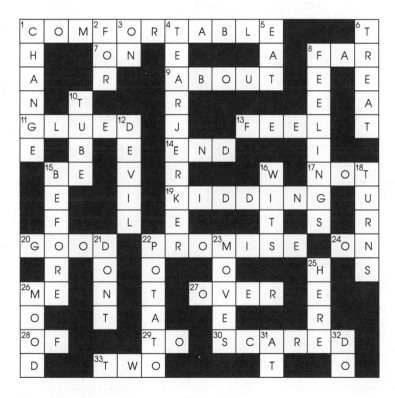

Guess the Idiom

1. you're pulling my leg
2. be glued to the tube
3. be on his mind
4. stand someone up
5. it's on me
6. take a break

Crossword Puzzle

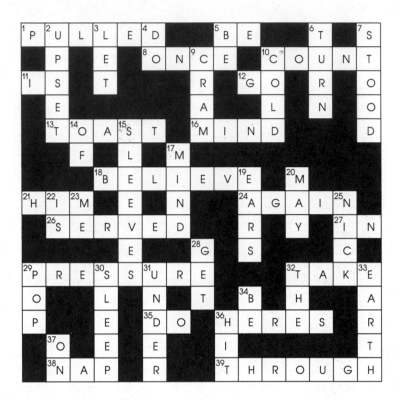

Guess the Idiom

1. be in hot water

2. hit the books

3. stay up

4. kill time

5. bend over backwards

6. give someone a hand

Alphabetical List of Idioms and Expressions

(The numbers refer to the lesson numbers in this book.)

A

(can/can't) afford **1**
(in/for) ages **2**
all day long **4**
all night long **4**

B

be a bookworm **5**
a mind reader **1**
a waste **10**
about ready **3**
bananas **3**
chicken **1**
divorced **1**
dying to **1**
engaged **1**
for sale **10**
glued to the tube **5**
going on **3**
guilty **11**
in a good/bad mood **5**
in good/bad shape **4**
in hot water **9**
in the mood **5**
in the same boat **4**
in the way **2**
in touch **2**
involved **5**
just about ready **3**
kidding **5**
married **1**
nuts **3**
off one's rocker **3**
on one's own **3**
on one's way **2**

on sale **10**
on *someone's* mind **6**
on the way **2**
out of breath **3**
out of one's mind **3**
out of the way **2**
out of touch **2**
over **9**
remarried **1**
scared out of one's wits **5**
scared to death **5**
separated **1**
sold out **10**
tongue-tied **3**
through **1**
under pressure **9**
upset **11**
up to **7**
before you know it **8**
bend over backwards **12**
bookworm **5**
break a promise **7**
break up **1**
bump into **2**
burn the midnight oil **9**
by oneself **3**

C

can/can't afford **1**
can/can't tell **1**
can't get over **11**
can't help **11**
can't stand **6**
can't stop **4**
care about **11**

157